words matter

Prayers from a Writer's Heart

robin lee hatcher

contents

meet robin

Best-selling novelist Robin Lee Hatcher is known for her heartwarming and emotionally charged stories of faith, courage, and love. She discovered her vocation after many years of reading everything she could put her hands on, including the backs of cereal boxes and ketchup bottles.

After fifteen years writing for the general fiction market and a change in her own heart, Robin began to write stories that included her Christian faith and values.

Winner of the Christy, the RITA, the Carol, the Inspirational Reader's Choice, and many other awards, she is also a recipient of the prestigious Lifetime Achievement Award from both Romance Writers of America (2001) and American Christian Fiction Writers (2014). Robin is the author of over 85 novels and novellas.

A lifelong Idahoan, Robin enjoys being with her family, spending time in the beautiful outdoors, reading books that make her cry, and watching romantic movies. Hobbies include Bible art journaling, decorative planning, and knitting. She makes her home on the outskirts of Boise, sharing it with a demanding Papillon dog and a persnickety tuxedo cat.

introduction

Hello from Idaho.

The book you are holding got its start in 2009 when I was asked to post prayers for writers to a large group of Christian novelists who meet via email. After I'd been posting my prayers for a few years, one of the leaders of the group said to me, "You should put those prayers into a book." I thought I might do so ... when I found the time.

We never find the time, do we? We have to make the time. A decade later, here it is at last, complete with prayers from 2009 up to 2022.

While most of the prayers you'll read in the following pages include requests for writers, they are above all prayers for anyone who loves Jesus and wants to serve Him. They are prayers that I needed to say for myself as well as for others. These are prayers from my heart, and perhaps they will reveal a little of who I am to those who read them.

As I went through the prayers in preparation for publishing this book, I discovered some from over a decade ago that sounded as if they could be referring to the more recent pandemic years. It was a reminder that there is nothing new under the sun. God held us then. He holds us now.

I separated out prayers used in special seasons or on a particular US holiday. But most of the prayers are unrelated to a time of the year.

However you choose to read this book, may the prayers and Scriptures you find within draw you ever closer to the Living Word. His name is Jesus.

In the grip of His grace,

Robin Lee Hatcher

prayer from a writer's heart

. . .

words matter!

Father God, remind us today how very important words are. You spoke this world into existence. And in Your image, we can speak life into those around us. Help us to be intentional in the words we speak. Help us to build up and not tear down.

Do the same with the words we write, with the stories we tell. There are plenty of books out there that can depress and darken the lives of readers. Help us to write stories that will give hope, stories that will offer truth and light.

Put a guard over our mouths (and our pens) when silence is the best response of all.

In Jesus' name we pray, Amen

---

do it all for him

Heavenly Father, today we thank You that You bless honest work. Thank You for calling us to serve You with our writing. Thank You for equipping us to do Your good work. Remind us today that in everything we do we work for You. Whether our words are read by few or by many, let us write for Your glory. Make us faithful to complete our tasks well.

That we may be better prepared for the demands of this day, remind us of the great work of Your Son. May Christ's sacrifice of love cause us to sacrifice for others. Put a guard over our mouths; make our words sweet to those who would hear them or read them.

Jesus, make us beautiful and powerful ambassadors for Your Kingdom. May our lives show a lost and politically correct world what being a Christian is truly about. Fill us with Your Holy Spirit and then let Your love flow out of us.

And Father God, would You bless and encourage our publishers, our editors, the folks who design our covers, all those who work in marketing and publicity, and every single sales rep. Would You strengthen and grow and bless Christian publishing in ways that we cannot even imagine.

In His name, Amen

---

write on our hearts

Bind [God's commandments] on your fingers; write them on the tablet of your heart. (Proverbs 7:3, NASB95)

Lord, without Your word written on the tablets of our hearts, we have absolutely nothing of any value to share with others. Do not allow us, in the busyness of our lives, to neglect making Your word a priority in our days.

Father, as we seek the stories You want us to tell, give us the wisdom and understanding that only You can impart. We live in troubled times. More troubled that we ever thought to see. We need wisdom as much as we need air. Help us to hear You, even when we are surrounded by the noise of this world.

Blessed be the name of the Lord. Amen

---

we surrender our writing

You whom I have taken from the ends of the earth, And called from its remotest parts And said to you, "You are My servant, I have chosen you and not rejected you. Do not fear, for I am with you; Do not anxiously look about you, for I am your God. I will strengthen you, surely I will help you, Surely I will uphold you with My righteous right hand." (Isaiah 41:9–10, NASB95)

Lord God, Holy Father, these are anxious times—in our nation, in this world, and in publishing.

Many of us have been writing for decades. Some have only started our publishing venture. But no matter where we are on our journey, the ground beneath our feet seems shifting and unsteady, and we don't always know where to turn or even how to stand still. Decisions about our careers that used to seem easy have become confusing and hard.

Lord, we surrender our writing to You today. It is You who gave us our gifts, our talents, in order to serve You. Our writing doesn't belong to us. It is Yours to do with as You will. Help us to hold it in an open hand and to be ready to say, "Yes," to You, no matter where You call us.

"Fear not!" Jesus said, again and again. Today we choose faith over fear. Today we choose trust over anxiety. Where You lead, Lord, we will follow. Where You lead, Lord, we will go.

In the mighty name of Jesus we pray, Amen

---

true disciples

And when day came, He called His disciples to Him and chose twelve of them, whom He also named as apostles ... and there was a large crowd of His disciples, and a great throng of people from all Judea ... (Luke 6: 12, 17, NASB95)

Father God, today we pray that, as writers, we won't simply be part of the great throng. Make us true disciples, those who learn directly from You and then are empowered to teach and disciple others. We live in a challenging time. Apart from You, we can do nothing that is truly worthwhile. Give us a hunger for Your word so that the words we write will have lasting value that can touch the hearts of our readers for Your kingdom.

For His glory and our joy, Amen

---

harbingers of hope

Therefore, those who had been scattered went about preaching the word. (Acts 8:4, NASB95)

Father God, this world we live in seems in total chaos. Viruses and violence abound. And so we turn to You.

Today we pray we would remember that the lives of the disciples were thrown into chaos due to persecution, and they were scattered to other parts of the world. Yet they went about sharing Jesus wherever they were. Help us today, through our lives, through our writing, through our interactions online, to share the truth of Jesus the Messiah. May we be harbingers of hope.

In this time when all of us long for a return to "normal," help us to know what needs to be maintained and held in a closed hand. Help us to cling to the Scriptures, to worship, to walking in the Spirit, to being disciples, and to discipling others. Likewise, help us to shake off those things that encumber us, familiar things that hamper our walk with You. And finally, help us to recognize those good things that we should hold with an open hand, offering them up to You to do with as You will.

Draw us close, Lord Jesus. We are Yours.

we need wisdom

But if any of you lacks wisdom, let him ask of God, who gives to all generously and without reproach, and it will be given to him. (James 1:5, NASB95)

Lord God, we live in a confusing age. We are bombarded by so-called information, but discerning the truth is a challenge. We need wisdom to make it through each and every day. You tell us that we need only ask of You, and You will generously supply wisdom without reproach. Today we ask.

Make us wise so that we might have the right words, both in our writing and in our speech. Grant us humility along with wisdom so that our words will be pleasing to the eyes and ears of others. Don't allow us to shy away from truth; therefore, make us bold as well.

In His name, Amen

we are wordsmiths

And a leper came to Him and bowed down before Him, and said, "Lord, if You are willing, You can make me clean." Jesus stretched out His

*hand and touched him, saying, "I am willing; be cleansed." And imme-
diately his leprosy was cleansed.* (Matthew 8:2–3, NASB95)

Dear Jesus, we know You are willing. Help us!!

Our country and our world are in a crisis because of an invisible enemy. First responders are working long hours and in tough conditions. Sick people need Your touch. Heal them, Lord. Grant those in authority wisdom. Help us, Jesus!!

Our country and our world are also sick for lack of knowing You and Your peace. Raise up Your church, Lord, in this time. Help us, Jesus!!

We are wordsmiths, Lord. You gave us a talent to touch people with words. As we write, as we use social media, as we talk to neighbors from across the street, give us the right words to bring comfort and encouragement to those within the reach of our words. People are afraid. Help us to be Your agents of calm. Stop us from spreading misinformation and instead to spread truth. Your truth. Truth with a capital "T."

Jesus, we can do nothing apart from You. Help us today. Help us this week. Comfort those who mourn. Bring healing to those who are sick.

In Your name we pray, Amen

---

bring beauty from ashes

*When I am afraid, I will put my trust in You ... You have taken
account of my wanderings; Put my tears in Your bottle. Are they not in
Your book?* (Psalm 56:3,8 NASB95)

Holy God, this we declare in faith: When we are afraid, we will put our trust in You.

There are some among us who are feeling afraid, alone,

forgotten. Remind us that we are seen by You, that You remember us and are with us. Draw us to Your word, Lord, where we will find pages and pages and pages filled with Your love for us. Even our tears are noted in Your book and saved in Your bottle.

For those of us in the midst of a storm, calm our hearts even if the wind remains strong. And if it be Your will, bring the storm to an end and help us see the promise of a new day.

We thank You, Lord, that You bring beauty from ashes. We thank You that You make everything work together for good for those who love You and are called according to Your purpose. Give us eyes to see You, whether we are in the valley or on the mountain top.

We ask it for Your glory, Amen

---

he sees

Behold, the eye of the LORD is on those who fear him, on those who hope in his steadfast love. (Psalm 33:18 ESV)

Father God, You see us. You know us inside and out. And You love us. It's hard to take in that truth sometimes. Remind us again. May we lie down and sleep in peace and wake up safely because we know You are watching over us. May we not fear, for You are with us. You hold us in Your righteous right hand. And keep us ever mindful that nothing, absolutely nothing, will separate us from Your love that is in Jesus our Messiah.

the one who has the answers

Father God, the world is in crisis. Sickness. People out of work. Nations politically divided. Riots. Destruction. Inequality. Injustice. As a people we have lost the ability to agree to disagree and instead differing ideas lead to hate and then more hate.

But we know You, Jesus, as Lord. We declare You are the One who has the answers, even for this time in which we find ourselves. It's confusing. It's heartbreaking. It's overwhelming. But we bow our knees to You, the King of kings and Lord of lords, and we ask for You to make a way in this wilderness.

We pray for those in authority, that they might act with wisdom. We pray for justice to prevail. We pray for a true peace.

Holy Spirit, we declare that You are welcome in this place. We humbly ask for an outpouring upon this broken land and this broken people. Help each one of us, all who follow the Christ, to make the invisible God visible to the world around us.

In the words of St. Francis:

> Lord, make me an instrument of your peace:
> where there is hatred, let me sow love;
> where there is injury, pardon;
> where there is doubt, faith;
> where there is despair, hope;
> where there is darkness, light;
> where there is sadness, joy.
>
> O divine Master, grant that I may not so much seek
> to be consoled as to console,
> to be understood as to understand,
> to be loved as to love.
> For it is in giving that we receive,
> it is in pardoning that we are pardoned,
> and it is in dying that we are born to eternal life.
> Amen.

hunger for his word

For the word of God is living and active, and sharper than any two-edged sword, even penetrating as far as the division of soul and spirit, of both joints and marrow, and able to judge the thoughts and intentions of the heart. (Hebrews 4:12, NASB2020)

Lord God, today we ask that You will place an ever-growing hunger in our hearts for Your written word. Make us people of Your Word so that the words we write will be infused with the truth. Change us as we read the Bible. Help us to see You with new eyes and worship You with new hearts. Refresh us, Holy Spirit, as we are living in an exhausting period of history. We are weary and our readers are weary. Help us to write stories that will lift readers up out of their trials and offer them the hope that only comes from knowing You.

In the mighty name of Yeshua, Amen

midst of storms

Father God, we pray today for those of us who are in the midst of the storms of life.

Sometimes those storms seem to go on forever, and we grow weary and even afraid. Remind us that You, Jesus, are here with us in a boat that is being tossed to and fro. Help us to be strong in You and to remember Your mighty power.

Remind us again that the joy of the Lord is our strength. The joy comes from our relationship with You, not from perfect circumstances.

Put a new song in our hearts today. A song of praise to You.

Restore to us the joy of knowing You, walking with You, talking with You, loving You.

In Jesus' beautiful, wonderful, powerful name we pray, Amen

---

let us not compromise

For Ezra had set his heart to study the law of the Lord and to practice it, and to teach His statutes and ordinances in Israel. (Ezra 7:10, NASB95)

Holy God, we pray today for those who call themselves followers of Christ to set their hearts to study Your word and to practice it. We pray that true believers won't be shaped and molded by the culture. We acknowledge that by following and practicing what You have told us to do, we will shape and mold our culture and our world. Help us not to compromise Your truth in order to fit in better or to avoid being an offense.

Change our minds and our hearts so that we will reflect You, Father, in Your holiness, in Your righteousness, in Your mighty power.

May the words that we write be right.

For His glory, Amen

---

your servants are listening

Speak, Lord, for Your servant is listening. (1 Samuel 3:9, NASB95)

Father God, we live in a noisy, noisy world. Although You can speak in ways that shake the foundations of creation, we know that You most often communicate in a still, small voice. In a whisper in our hearts. Help us to learn to be still so that we can hear You. Help us to tune out the constant noise of our 21st century lives. Help us to opt out of email and social media and television and podcasts for a period of time where we can simply listen to You.

Lord, You have given us a gift, an ability to communicate with others through storytelling, through our writing. But if we can't hear You, if we don't listen to Your voice, we have nothing of value to share with readers.

Speak, Lord, for Your servants are listening.

---

we have tribulation

These things I have spoken to you, so that in Me you may have peace. In the world you have tribulation, but take courage; I have overcome the world. (John 16:33, NASB95)

Lord Jesus, there has been another mass shooting in the US, this time in a small church in a tiny town. Our hearts cry, How can someone do that, Lord? But we know how. We know that, until You return in Your glory, evil still roams this earth, taking down those it can, causing havoc wherever it might.

Jesus, we will have tribulation in this world, but we can take heart because You have overcome the world. Remind each of us of that truth. Remind each member of the small congregation of that truth. Send other Christians to wrap their arms around the grieving.

As we write our stories today, remind us again of the power and importance of words, and let the words we write lift and encourage rather than tear down and defeat.

In Christ's name, Amen

comfort or disturb?

Father God, as shown in Acts 4, You frequently comfort the disturbed (those trapped in sin or sickness or poverty, etc.) and You frequently disturb the comfortable (the Sadducees and Pharisees and the proud and the self-assured, etc.).

Wherever You find us today, Lord, whether we need to be disturbed or comforted or both, would You make our hearts tender toward the leading of Your Holy Spirit. Guide us, Lord, that we might be true lights for You in a very dark world.

Blessed be Your name. Amen

shaped by the spirit

Therefore I, the prisoner of the Lord, implore you to walk in a manner worthy of the calling with which you have been called, with all humility and gentleness, with patience, showing tolerance for one another in love, being diligent to preserve the unity of the Spirit in the bond of peace. (Ephesians 4:1–3, NASB95)

Father God, we are a world badly in need of unity of the Spirit. We know that this world can never know true peace apart from faith in Jesus Christ, but Your word calls us to have peace within the body. And so this is what we pray for today. We ask for the gift of discernment to be spread across the world to Your faithful followers. We ask that You would give all of us a hunger to feast on Your written word. We ask for an outpouring of the gift of faith, that You would raise up a church that stands for Truth. We ask for the gift of wisdom.

We are writers. We are lovers of the written word. God, help us to use those passions for Your glory and don't allow us to be shaped by the culture but to be shaped by Your Holy Spirit, from the inside out.

Lord, we know that You have kept a remnant in every generation. But we pray for more than a remnant. We pray for a mighty army that will stand for You, clothed in the full armor of God.

In Jesus' name we pray, Amen

---

what is truth?

Pilate asked, "What is truth?" And whether or not he wanted an answer, we declare that we want one. We want to find our way through the deceptions of this world and our own sinful natures. We are so adept at justification and layering our own thoughts over what You tell us in Your word and calling that truth.

Jesus, You are the Way, the Truth, and the Life. This we proclaim.

We are writers, Lord. You have made us storytellers. Help us to tell stories that will glorify You and that will speak Your truth into a hurting and confused world. Protect us from deception—from the enemy, from our culture, from what simply makes us feel good because it is easier. Help us to take up our crosses daily and follow You.

Amen

---

multiply our efforts

When we live in a generous posture, it brings out generosity in others.
— Trevor Estes, Pastor, VCF Boise

Jesus, on the day that You fed the 5,000, You and Your disciples had gone away to rest and be alone. Your heart was grieved over the news that John the Baptist had been arrested. And yet, when the crowds sought You out, You did not reject them. When they grew hungry, You did not send them off to buy food for themselves as Your disciples recommended (a perfectly reasonable suggestion). You were moved with compassion. You taught, healed, and satisfied their hunger. Your compassion surpassed human economy. It went beyond the bare minimum. The natural resources of a few loaves and fishes were stretched supernaturally as Your disciples moved out in obedience.

Move us in compassion and obedience today, Lord. Don't allow us to be fearful of whether or not we have the time margins or the financial margins to meet the needs that we see. Move us out in faith, and let us see You multiply our efforts supernaturally.

The world around us is hungry. Many live daily, not knowing if they will eat today or tomorrow or the next day. Many live daily without spiritual food either. Help us to offer both, not either/or. Help us to look upon the crowds with the compassion of Jesus in our hearts.

Help us to write words that will feed the thousands—men, women, and children—and then spur others to action.

In Your mighty name we pray, Amen

we trust you

Though the fig tree does not blossom and there is no fruit on the vines, [though] the product of the olive fails and the fields yield no food, though the flock is cut off from the fold and there are no cattle in the stalls, Yet I will rejoice in the Lord; I will exult in the [victorious] God of my salvation! The Lord God is my Strength, my personal bravery,

and my invincible army; He makes my feet like hinds' feet and will
make me to walk [not to stand still in terror, but to walk] and make
[spiritual] progress upon my high places [of trouble, suffering, or
responsibility]! For the Chief Musician; with my stringed instruments.
(Habakkuk 3:17–19, AMP)

Father God, sometimes our writing feels like a wasteland. Maybe
it's been rejected by an editor or a reader. Maybe it's because we
need to add more motivation or more color to our characters.
Maybe it's because we haven't ramped up the tension enough
and the plot feels flat, even to us, the writers.

For those of us feeling as if we are in a wasteland, for those of
us who find ourselves where the fig tree doesn't blossom and
there is no fruit on the vine, please remind us, Lord, to stop and
rejoice in You. You are our strength. You are our personal
bravery and our invincible army. You will make us walk upon
high places. We trust in You.

may our words bear fruit

Father God, today we pray that every one of us will be filled
with the knowledge of Your will. Grant us spiritual wisdom and
understanding so that the way we live and the words we write
will be worthy of You. May our novels please You in all respects,
and may they bear fruit as they go out to readers. Protect us from
the false doctrines, perverted worldviews, and deceptive
philosophies that bombard us daily. Fill us with the true mystery
of God which is Jesus Christ Himself. (Colossians 1 & 2)

In His name, Amen

creativity is no accident

Father in Heaven, You are a creative God. You created the earth. You created the sun, moon, and stars. You created the animals. And You created all mankind. Not only that, but You created us in Your image. And just one of the things that means is that You created us to be creators. You created us to be creative, like You. Amazing, Lord!!

It is no accident that we long to write. It is no accident that we want to paint or draw or take photographs or knit or crochet or make a thousand different things in a thousand different ways. You put that desire in us when You made us in Your image.

Help us to use those gifts, those traits, those reflections of You in ways that bring glory to You and to Your kingdom. Help us to use them to make a difference here on earth as we live out our lives between the first and second advents. Your kingdom has broken through, but we still live in an imperfect world troubled by sin. Help us to shine light on those places where darkness exists.

Let the words of our mouths (and the words of our pens, typewriters, and computers) and the meditations of our hearts be acceptable in Your sight, O Lord, our rock and our Redeemer.

---

have mercy

Holy, holy, holy God. We lift up our nation before You. You have called Your church to love. You have also called Your church to speak truth, no matter what the culture around us says. You have called Your church to be holy as You are holy.

By the power of Your Spirit, guide us in the righteous path. You have called upon us to deny ourselves, to cast off the sin that so easily entangles us, to take up our crosses, and to follow You.

You have called us to purity, but our culture says things are okay that You say are not. Too often the church mirrors the world around us. Forgive us and cleanse us. Help us to be loving examples of living for God and not to please ourselves or others.

We are a nation and a world in chaos, Father. Have mercy. Lord, have mercy.

giver of gifts

Sometimes we have to be willing to give something up to God in order to get it back from God … God will test us to make sure the gift isn't more important than the Gift Giver, the dream isn't more important to us than the Dream Giver. — Mark Batterson in *Draw the Circle*

Father God, Giver of gifts, Giver of dreams, we thank You today for the gift of writing which You bestowed upon us. We thank You for the dreams You have placed in our hearts and minds. We want to write words that give You glory. We want to write books that will bring You pleasure. We want to write to change the world by changing hearts, one reader at a time.

But Lord, we don't want our gifts and dreams to be more important than You in our lives. Don't let us make idols of our stories. Don't let us want our books in print more than we want You. Set us free from our own ideas of what we should do so that we can choose the path You want each one of us to take.

Jesus, be Lord over every aspect of our hearts and lives, we pray.

In Your name, Amen

none like you

For the word of the cross is foolishness to those who are perishing, but to us who are being saved it is the power of God … For I am determined to know nothing among you except Jesus Christ, and Him crucified. (1 Corinthians 1:18 and 2:2, NASB95)

Holy God, we begin our work by proclaiming You are God. There is none like You. We thank You that the good news of salvation in Christ Jesus reached us and opened our hearts to Your love. We want to share that love with others as You have called us to do.

We are determined, Lord, to know nothing except Jesus Christ, and Him crucified. That is foolishness to much of the world. It is foolishness even to members within our own families. But because of Your salvation, we know that it is the very power of God in our lives.

Thank You, Father, that when we are weak, then You are strong.

begin with praise

Lord God, today we bring a sacrifice of praise! Not only our voices. We offer our lives to You as living sacrifices. Make us truly thankful for all of the blessings in our lives, even when big problems try to overwhelm us and hide the blessings from our notice. You are worthy of our praise, no matter our circumstances. Holy, holy, holy is the Lamb of God.

Amen

walk on water

And He said, "Come!" And Peter got out of the boat, and walked on the water and came toward Jesus. (Matthew 14:29, NASB95)

Lord Jesus, today we ask You for God-sized dreams and for the faith to get out of the boat and walk on water whenever You look at us and say, "Come!" Please don't let us be content to sit in the boat, whether out of fear or out of practicality or because we haven't learned to trust You for the impossible.

Father God, we lay down our disappointments today and we take up our trust in You to do everything You have promised to do. We do not have because we do not ask. Therefore, Holy One, we are asking in faith to see You move in our lives in unexpected ways. Don't let us be satisfied with lives that only achieve what we can accomplish under our own intellect and effort.

Give us a big vision, Lord. Give us a new vision. Help us to dream of lives that can only happen through Your will and Your might. We want to walk on water with our eyes set on You.

In the mighty name of Jesus we pray, Amen

made complete

Holy God, we live in the time of the "now" and "not yet." Your Kingdom has come to the earth, and yet it has not fully come. Evil still roams about, seeking to devour and destroy. Help us to put on the armor You have provided to us.

You have commissioned Your people, those who have received Christ Jesus the Lord, to walk in Him. We are to be firmly rooted and built up in Jesus. Establish us in the faith, O Most High. Help us to receive Your instructions. Cause us to overflow with thanksgiving.

Father, protect us from being taken captive through a mistaken worldview or any empty deception, according to the traditions of men. Shield us from the elementary principles of this world and instead shower us in the principles of Christ. Help us to take them deep into our hearts and to live by them.

Yeshua, make Your church strong wherever we are planted. May we reflect Your glory. May You be seen and heard in us.

In You, Lord, we have been made complete. You are the head over all rule and authority, and we submit our lives, our thoughts, our work, our homes, our families, and all that is important to us to You today.

Amen

the battle is his

Lord, what a beautiful world You created. Even after the fall of man and the curse upon the earth that came with it, we see the beauty of Your handiwork all around us in all seasons.

Father, on this day, would You encourage us as we write our stories. Finding the right words isn't always easy. Sometimes it seems impossible. Help us to hear You and not the voices of doubt, voices that shout at us and call us failures. Help us to reject the lies and to hear Your still small voice.

And Lord, when we are attacked cruelly because of our faith and trust in You, we ask that You give us the strength to stand. Help us to rise up in truth and to remember the battle is Yours.

In Christ's mighty name, Amen

rule over us

Just as you are rich in everything—in faith and speech, in knowledge and all sincerity, and in the love we have shown among you—now I ask you to invest richly in this gracious work too. (2 Corinthians 8:7, the Voice Bible)

Lord God, we worship You on this beautiful day, whether beautiful means warm or cold, sunny or cloudy, calm or windy. It is beautiful because You created this world and because You created each one of us.

Father, You have placed the desire to write in the hearts of many who are reading this prayer. Moreover, we have the desire to please You in the work of our hands. Help us, Lord, to invest ourselves richly in the gracious work You have given us to accomplish. Don't allow us to offer You anything but our very best.

We ask a special blessing today on all of the publishing professionals with whom we work. Upon our agents, upon our editors, upon the salesmen and the marketers and the publicists and the art directors and staff. Would You encourage all who have anything to do with getting our stories into the hands of readers. Would You draw them closer to Yourself.

Keep us close, too, Jesus. Help us to see and write truth, to be ready pens in Your hands to spread Your truth. *You* are the truth, O mighty King. Rule over our hearts today.

---

he hears us

[Jesus said,] "Father, I am grateful that You have heard Me." (John 11:41, The Voice Bible)

Father God, how wonderful it is to know, deep in our bones, that You hear us when we talk to You. Sometimes, our prayers feel as if they go no higher than the ceiling. But since You are near, since You are leaning in to hear us, that doesn't matter, does it? Thank You. Thank You.

Lord, it doesn't matter if we believe You called us to be writers or if we believe we write in order to fulfill the calling to follow You. Either way, we write our stories, hoping to reach readers, hoping to give them a few hours of enjoyment, hoping even to encourage them in some small way. Being a writer has never been an easy career choice, but it can feel especially hard for those who have published and then had that option taken away. Would You comfort, guide, and encourage those who feel that way today.

Father, we know You hear us. Now help us to hear You. Don't allow us to become so embroiled in the busyness and business of living that we become deaf to Your still small voice.

Grant us today a burst of creativity, and let the words that we write glorify our Creator.

In Jesus' name, Amen

white as snow

Lord, we'd like to take a moment to put our cares aside and simply focus on You.

You have loved us so much that Jesus died for us. How can we not be overwhelmed by that truth? Because we have put our trust in what Jesus accomplished on the cross, we will spend eternity in Your presence. Amazing!

Thank You for being a God of second chances, of new beginnings, of fresh and ever-changing seasons. The blood of Christ has washed us white as snow. For some of us in the world today, we may be able to look out our windows on a chilly, snowy day and see exactly how white that is. Awesome!

You are the Alpha and Omega, the First and the Last, the Beginning and the End. You are Counselor, Comforter, Provider, our Strong Tower.

Help us to make space for You to move in our lives today. Help us to be satisfied in Your presence.

We love You, Lord, and we lift our voices in praise.

so sick of words

Father God, there are days when we sit down to write that we feel like Eliza Doolittle in *My Fair Lady* when she sings that she's sick of words. It feels as if we're putting words on paper that mean nothing, words that are wooden and dead, words that prove we are hacks or, worse, boring.

What made us think we should spend a good portion of our lives spinning stories to entertain others?

Forgetting those feelings, Lord, today we declare in faith that we will do the very best we can with the talent You gave us and with the craft that we have tried so hard to learn. We will not let those voices of doubt keep us from doing the work You have called us to, whether for this one book or for a hundred more.

In the mighty name of Jesus, Amen

spoken into existence

Father God, You spoke the world into existence. Your Son is identified as the Word. Words seem to have great importance to You. Would You help us to give them great importance in our lives as well. Increase our love for Your written word, and when we write, help us to write words that will be to Your glory. Keep us from speaking or writing carelessly.

Lord, You have bestowed gifts of the Spirit upon Your children. Rekindle those gifts within us today. Make us aware of them and help us to use them according to Your will.

Father, help us to be a people of prayer. Deepen our times with You. Make us keenly aware of Your presence in every moment of our days. Help us to rejoice in hope, persevere in tribulation, practice hospitality, bless those who persecute us, rejoice with those who rejoice, and weep with those who weep. So much as it depends upon us, help us to be at peace with all mankind.

Words matter, Lord, and so we offer ours to You this day.

To God be the glory, Amen

let that song well up

Father God, we come to you today, and we ask that You would pour out Your anointing upon the stories that we write. And as we write our stories, Lord, would You remind us afresh of all the blessings You have given us so generously. We thank You that Your deserved wrath and anger fell upon Jesus in our stead. We are so thankful for Your mercy and grace. We will trust in You and not be afraid of what today or tomorrow or next week or next month or next year will bring with it.

Jesus, You are our strength and our song. Would You let that song well up in our hearts today and spill over upon those around us. Would you embolden us to share You with a downtrodden and discouraged world.

And Lord, for those of us who find ourselves staring at a deadline that will arrive all too soon, would You multiply our efforts and our words, granting us a renewed enthusiasm for our projects and with divine inspiration.

We thank You, Lord, for this day because it is the day that You have made. We will rejoice and be glad in it.

In Christ's mighty name, Amen

---

blow us where you will

[Jesus said,] "The wind blows where it wishes and you hear the sound of it, but do not know where it comes from and where it is going; so is everyone who is born of the Spirit." (John 3:8, NASB95)

Jesus, today we pray that the wind of Your Holy Spirit will blow us where You will. Whether it be a soft breeze or a mighty storm, Your disciples want to go where You would have us go and do what You would have us do.

If there are dead leaves of sin or discouragement or lifestyle choices clinging to our limbs, send Your wind to blow them away.

If the fire of our zeal for You has cooled, send Your wind to rekindle the flame.

Revive us, Lord, and send us forth with Your winds filling our sails.

Amen

---

renew the passion

Lord, we get so caught up in our culture's crazy thinking some-times. Today, would You make us more cognizant of the harsh realities in the rest of the world. Would You help us to think of ourselves less and think of others more. For those of us who are married, help us to serve our spouses. For those of us who are parents, help us to be examples of righteous living to our children. For those of us who are alone, help us to reach out to the truly lonely.

Father God, teach us to be true and faithful disciples of Jesus the Messiah. Don't let us settle for sliding into heaven by the skin of our teeth, glad that we prayed that sinner's prayer. Help us to pour ourselves out right up to our last moment on earth.

May the words that we write and the words that we speak be what You would have us write and speak. May those words go forth and not return void because You have blessed them for success in this crazy, upside-down world. Renew the passion we once felt in regard to our mission on earth as Christians.

In His name we pray, Amen

your will be done

Father, sometimes the numbers (or lack thereof) in this publishing business beat us down. Sales numbers. Social media numbers. Bestseller rankings.

We feel like failures. We want to crawl away and lick our wounds. We try our best not to ask "Why?" but then we ask it anyway. Why is that writer selling a gazillion copies and we've sold ten ... on ebook ... for 99 cents? We're like Peter looking over his shoulder at John and saying, "What about him?"

Well, Lord, today we want to lay those "whys" and all of our petty and not-so-petty complaints at Your feet. Today we want to pray the one prayer that every disciple of Jesus the Messiah must learn to pray: Your will be done.

Your will be done, Lord. Your will be done.

i will do as you say

When [Jesus] had finished speaking, He said to Simon, "Put out into the deep water and let down your nets for a catch." Simon answered and said, "Master, we worked hard all night and caught nothing, but I will do as You say and let down the nets." (Luke 5:5, NASB95)

Lord Jesus, may our response to Your voice be like Peter's. "But I will do as You say." May that be our response even when what You tell us to do doesn't make sense to our rational mind. Your word tells us we will be known by our fruit, and that we cannot call You "Master" and not do as You say.

Master, we want to bear good fruit. Help us to hear Your voice and to act upon it.

"Yes, Lord!"

---

so many are hungry

Beloved Savior, when You walked this earth, You fed thousands of people with five loaves and two fish. You blessed the food. The disciples served the people. And the people ate and were satisfied.

We are Your disciples, Lord. You have called us to serve in a world that is broken by sin, a world that eats unblessed food and isn't satisfied. So many are still hungry because they don't know that You are the Bread of Life.

You have given us truth in Your written word, Jesus. Help us today to incorporate Your truth into the stories we write. Don't let us squander whatever talent You have given us. Help us to touch and lift hearts. Help us to love as You love. Help us to follow You daily in all that we say and do.

Amen

rejoice in the day he's made

This is the Lord's doing; It is marvelous in our eyes. This is the day which the Lord has made; Let us rejoice and be glad in it. (Psalm 118:23–24, NASB95)

Father God, a writer's life can be topsy-turvy at times. And lately it seems more so than ever. For years and years, we could tell others what publishing "looked like." That's no longer true. We don't know what it will look like next year. We don't know what it will look like next month. Or tomorrow.

Lord, remind us that You are in control. That whatever tomorrow brings, You haven't left us or forgotten us. Give us courage to face change, something many of us resist as our first instinct.

Jesus, in faith we choose to rejoice and be glad in the day that You have made.

In Your holy name, Amen

be still

Lord, some days we feel as if we are being crushed beneath deadlines. Writing deadlines. Children's schedules. Obligations to our churches. Commitments to friends. Needs of our spouses. The phone rings and rings. The emails fill our inboxes. The hour hand on the clock seems to be moving in double time.

Be still and know that I am God.
Help us today to cease striving and to find our rest in You.
Be still and know that I am God.

Your name, O Lord, is our Strong Tower. We run into it and are not afraid.

Be still and know that I am God.

Help us this day to be a bright light in a dark world.

Be still and know that I am God.

Our trust is in You alone, Jesus, our King.

---

reflections

Lord God, we acknowledge today that we reflect the God whom we perceive. Our words and actions are a direct result of who we believe You to be. Who we really believe You to be, deep down in our very core.

Jesus, don't let us be satisfied with surface belief. Don't let us craft idols that are cold and speechless and lifeless. Let the truths of who You are—Holy, Just, Loving, Almighty, our Champion, our Provider, the First and the Last, the Ancient of Days, the King of kings, the Lamb of God, the Resurrection, our Comforter —go down deep and take root within us.

Give us keen perception, and let us reflect who You truly are to others around us, to all who see us or hear us, to all who read the words that we write.

Make it so, Lord Jesus. Amen

---

move out in faith

Father God, You have known us from before time. You know that as creative beings we have had big dreams, huge hopes, for the stories that we write.

Some of us are fairly new to the publishing business. Some of us have been at it for decades. Some of us have known success.

Some of us feel like we've been kicked around the block a few times.

What is Your plan for our writing, Lord? We perish without vision. Your word tells us so. We boldly ask today for the special vision You have for our lives and for the books we write.

Give us courage as well as physical and mental stamina to do the work and to do it well. Don't let us skate by, giving to You something that cost us nothing. We trust You, Father, even when You lead us along rocky pathways, pathways that are new to us. We confess that we are more comfortable with the familiar, even when it isn't where we want to be, even when we know it isn't where You want us to be. Help us to not be afraid of fresh visions for the future. Help us to move out in faith.

For those who have lost complete sight of the joy of writing, would You restore that today, Lord.

In the holy name of Jesus we pray, Amen

walk in truth

Abba Father, as writers, we read or hear both criticisms of our work and praise for our work. Help us not to be crushed by the former. Help us not to be made proud by the latter.

Help us to remember that all that matters is what *You* say about us. Help us to find our satisfaction in Christ alone. The world tells us what success is, but as Your children, we know most of it is smoke and mirrors and unimportant in the light of eternity.

Help us to keep Christ and His cross before us today. And help us to remember that *we* are Your masterpieces. You have written stories that matter into our lives. Stories that will last for eternity. Help us to walk in that truth this week.

In Him we pray, Amen

we invite his will

This is the confidence which we have before Him, that, if we ask anything according to His will, He hears us. And if we know that He hears us in whatever we ask, we know that we have the requests which we have asked from Him. (1 John 5:14–15)

Father God, when we pray, would You make us better listeners and not just talkers.

Father, when we don't see the answers we want on the timetable we want, would You keep us from doubting Your word. Would You help us to ask You why we doubt, and if there is sin in our lives, would You help us to repent of it.

Lord, when we don't know Your will, would You help us to *invite* Your will. Would You burn into our hearts the willingness to pray, as Mary prayed: "... may it be done to me according to Your word."

Jesus, we bow down to You today and bless Your holy name.

wielders of words

O Eternal One, what is man, that You even care to know him? or the son of man, that You are mindful of him? Humans are like a passing breath; their time on earth is like a shadow that passes over us during the day and soon is gone. (Psalm 144:3-4, The Voice Bible)

Holy God, most precious Lord, help us to remember when life is hard or confusing or scary that no matter what else happens, You are still Almighty, Omniscient, Loving, Kind, All-Powerful. You are the First and the Last, the Beginning and the End.

Lord, You put power into words. As wielders of words, help us never to lead others astray from the truth by failing to know Your Word intimately ourselves. Don't let us misrepresent You with the words we write. Remind us that it isn't our choice to decide who You are. Open our hearts and our minds to hear the Shepherd's voice.

Guard us, Lord. Guard our minds and hearts and spirits. Help us to be holy as You are Holy. Keep our faith from being distorted by our culture and the times we live in. Instead help us to be molded by the Potter's hands for His purpose and plan.

We are here for but a moment in time, Lord. Make our lives count for something. Cause us to write stories that can reach the world for You.

Amen and Amen

in the hallway

Father God, today we thank You for Your sons and daughters who are co-laborers with us in the Christian writing community. We thank You that they have answered the call to follow Jesus, and in doing so, they have entrusted and dedicated the work of their hands to Your glory.

Would You help each one of us today to willingly give of our time and our talents to further Your kingdom. Would You cause us to give the very best that we have. Would You remind us that we may be the only Bible others in our spheres will ever "read." May Your word be seen in us. For those who are discouraged, would You provide encouragement. For those who are weary, would You cause them to rise up on wings of eagles.

Someone once said, "When God closes a door, He opens another. But it's hell in the hallway."

Father, we know there are some reading this prayer who are

in the hallway, waiting for another door to open. Would You give them peace and comfort while they wait for Your direction, for the opening of a door for them to step through.

Bless the words that we write today. May they glorify You and shed light into the darkness.

Amen

---

beloved children

Consider the kind of extravagant love the Father has lavished on us— He calls us children of God! It's true; we are His beloved children. And in the same way the world didn't recognize Him, the world does not recognize us either. (1 John 3:1, NASB95)

Abba Father, today we pray that we will pause in our "doing" and spend some time simply "being." You have declared us Your beloved children. What a miracle that is, that we are Yours because of the shed blood of Jesus. That we can come to You without fear. That when we fall You pick us up and dust us off and set us on our feet again.

We are strangers in a strange land, Lord. All around us is the allure of pleasure and the passion to possess things—things, things, and more things. Would You focus our thoughts today not on pleasure or possessions but upon Your Son. Would You remind us that we need to see the world through Your eyes and not to see You through the world's eyes.

And Father, we are writers. Would You remind us today of the importance You put upon words. We are surrounded by images in magazines, on TV, on the big screen. But You spoke things into existence. Jesus came into the world as the Word. Words matter to You and they matter in a hurting world. Would You help us to write truth. Would You help us to write words that honor You. Our attempts will never be all we hope for, but would You make them what You will.

In the name of Jesus, the Messiah, we pray, Amen

words matter to us

Abba Father, we are writers, a people of words. Words matter to us. How we string them together. How they affect our readers.

But Lord, our words are temporary. Only Your words are eternal. Only Your words go forth and never return void. Give us a passionate desire to know Your written word. Your word is our daily bread. Don't let us choose to go hungry when a feast is readily at hand.

To God be the glory, Amen

a day late

Lord, here we are, "a day late and a dollar short," as the saying goes. Does everyone in today's crazy world feel that way? Some might want to yell, "Stop the world. I want to get off!"

So, Lord, would You quiet our thoughts. Would You still our hearts. Would You open our eyes and ears. Help us to look away from the death and chaos that is happening in the world. Help us to forget, if only for a short while, the demands of deadlines and loved ones. Help us to free ourselves from the constant call of social networking. We want to be still and know You.

Paul, who served You diligently for decades, even to the point of death, wrote late in his ministry, "I want to know Christ." Remind us that we always need to know You more, Jesus. Help us not to fall captive to our culture. Help us not to see You through the eyes of this world but through the truth of Your word.

And Father God, please protect Your children who are serving as missionaries around the world, many in very dangerous countries.

Blessed be Your name, Amen

---

we're a family

Give thanks to the Lord, for He is good; For His lovingkindness is ever-lasting. (Psalm 118:1, NASB95)

Father God, we thank You. You are always good. You have never ceased to be loving and kind. You invite us to come and join You. You invite us to bring our concerns and to lay them at Your feet.

You have made those who trust in Christ a family that is called "the church." Sometimes we are a fractured family, but even then we *are* family. You have called us to love one another. And narrowing down, You have made those of us in the writing community who profess You as Sovereign Lord into a family as well. Would You help us to see each writer through the eyes of Christ's love for them. Would You help us to remember that we are called to prefer one another, to serve one another.

In Jesus' name we pray, Amen

---

mourning into dancing

You are my shelter, O Eternal One—my soul's sanctuary! Shield me from shame; rescue me by Your righteousness. Hear me, Lord! Turn

Your ear in my direction. Come quick! Save me! Be my rock, my shelter, my fortress of salvation! (Psalm 31:1-2, The Voice Bible)

Lord, today we pray especially for those writers who are struggling with discouragement, with disappointments, with fears about the future. Would You turn their mourning into dancing this day. Would You lift their burden and make them ever aware that You are willing and waiting and wanting to carry it for them.

Father God, make us mindful that "conditional trust" isn't trust at all. Help us to truly trust You even when the thing we fear most arrives on our doorsteps. At the end of all of our fears, at the end of our greatest disappointments, at the end of our "if only," we find … THEN GOD.

Lord, You are the Beginning and the End. You are the Alpha and Omega. You are the First and the Last. You are the answer to our heart's cry, to our deepest doubts, to our greatest terrors. Take our hands, Lord. In You we will put our trust, no matter what.

kept for jesus

To those who are the called, beloved in God the Father, and kept for Jesus Christ. (Jude 1b, NASB95)

Father God, how amazing it is to know that we have been called to faith in Jesus by You. How incredible it is that we are loved by You. How secure we feel knowing that You keep us safe, for Jesus and in Jesus.

Lord, may the truth of this verse go deep into our hearts and, from it, may we write words of truth that will impact our world. You have called the church to be Your hands and feet on this earth until Jesus returns. You have called us to speak to the mountains and see them move. Some problems in this world seem too big, but we acknowledge that nothing is too big for You and that small things can make a huge difference.

Be with us today as we write. Whether we are writing a blog post or an article or a scene in a novel, help us to give our very best and then to offer it up to You.

Amen

---

new victories

Father God, we pray today for a fresh touch from You. Help us to abide in Christ, day by day, moment by moment. Don't let us be satisfied with the victories of yesterday or the words You spoke to us a year ago or a month ago or a week ago.

Help us to turn our ears to You to hear from You *now*. Help us to march forth to achieve new victories today. We want to be useful in Your kingdom.

And Lord, there are those, even within the body of Christ, who disdain the books and ministries of Christian writers. Your word tells us that if we suffer for the sake of righteousness, we are blessed. Help us to focus our hearts and minds on You, and to let the rest roll off of us without leaving traces of anger or discouragement.

Don't let us grow weary of doing good. Don't let us grow weary of following You where You lead us individually and corporately.

In Christ's name we pray, Amen

---

lord, build the house

Unless the LORD builds the house, They labor in vain who build it;
Unless the LORD guards the city, The watchman keeps awake in vain.
(Psalm 127:1, NASB95)

Lord God, we don't want our labor on our books to be in vain. Writing and revising and editing and marketing are too hard for it all to end up meaningless. But we need You, Lord, to build it. We want our stories to be of the very best quality. We want our stories to be ones that please You and that You can use. We want our books to touch hearts and bring readers closer to You, Jesus. We want the same of our blog posts and our interactions with friends and strangers on Facebook and whatever else we write or speak. And for that to happen, we must allow You to build the house.

Lord, build the house of our lives. Whatever You want our lives to be, Lord, build them that way.

Lord, build the house of our marriages. Make them the kind of shelters that You desire. Put their foundation down deep in Your word.

Lord, build the house of our careers. Don't let us compare ourselves or our work to others. Keep our hearts and minds looking at Jesus.

Lord, remind us again that a good harvest in this life is not due to endless toil but to Your blessing. Even while we sleep.

"It is vain for you to rise up early, To retire late, To eat the bread of painful labors; For He gives to His beloved even in his sleep." (Psalm 127:2, NASB95)

Amen and Amen

let us hear his whisper

Father God, as writers, we spend a great deal of time searching for the perfect words to describe what we want to convey to readers. We wonder how much time You spend trying to convey Your love for us and we are too busy to read what You have written, too busy to hear the words You speak to those who have ears to hear.

And so we pray that we would pause for a moment and listen for Your whisper in our hearts, that we would stop our hectic thoughts and hectic lives and let ourselves feel Your arms around us.

Lord, there is so much trouble in this world, so many people we need to pray for, so much despair and death. Help us to stand on a hill and hold Your light high. Help us to be Your hands and feet on the earth. Help us to live rightly in this time between Jesus' first and second coming. The kingdom has come and yet the kingdom has not fully come. We live in the "now but not yet."

Help us to boldly follow where You lead us. Whether we are young or old, don't let us become satisfied and comfortable when there is so much to be done, even right in our own neighborhoods.

In Your name, Amen

not easy to live with a writer

Father God, help us to write words and stories that reveal Your truth. Help us to lean in close to You so that we can hear Your heartbeat for a hurting world. Help us not to compare ourselves or our stories to others. Help us to be concerned with what You are doing in our own lives, in our own books, in our own careers. Help us to remember that You have a very specific and individual plan for each of us. Let us walk in that purpose and plan in joy.

Lord, today we pray for those who love us, especially family members or friends who share our household. We know it isn't easy to live with a writer. We know our imaginations can take us far away even when we are physically present. Would You remind us that it's the relationships in our lives that are the most important. Help us to be sensitive and loving.

Jesus, we want to serve You with all of our beings and to love You with all of our hearts.

We ask it all in Your name, Amen

---

what a mystery

So that Christ may dwell in your hearts through faith; and that you, being rooted and grounded in love, may be able to comprehend with all the saints what is the breadth and length and height and depth, and to know the love of Christ which surpasses knowledge, that you may be filled up to all the fullness of God. (Ephesians 3:17–19, NASB95)

Father God, how amazing is Your love toward us. What a mystery it can be, even to those of us who have trusted in You for our salvation. The love of Jesus surpasses knowledge.

Today we pray that all who read this prayer would be rooted and grounded not only in Your love but in right doctrine as well. The world pulls and tugs at us. The enemy of our souls whispers half-truths in our ears, half-truths that so often sound like truth. If we are to write Your truths for a hurting world, we must know Your truth in our minds and in our hearts. Help us to be students of Your word. Plant in us a passion to know You more. Keep us from being tossed to and fro by the storms of life. Help us to reflect Your glory to all who see us and to all who read our books.

In the glorious name of Your Son, Amen

***

speak in new ways

Abba Father, Most Holy God, why is it so many of us begin our days already feeling behind? Maybe it's because life seems to be going faster and faster and faster.

Today, we pray that each one of us will offer our most urgent concerns to You. Help us to hold those concerns lightly and to release them into Your care. Help us to relax into Your love for us. Help us to not only listen for Your voice but to be prepared to hear You speak to us in new ways.

Lord, there are brothers and sisters in our midst who are hurting today. Would You give them a special measure of comfort right now.

And Father, would You help us to write words that are true and powerful and that make a difference in the world around us. We are surrounded by sin and evil and danger while here on earth, but we are asking for Your kingdom to break through today.

For Your glory and our joy, Amen

***

in our daddy's arms

Abba Father, Wonderful God, Mighty Savior, some of us are so tired of the storms that batter us, day after day. Some may even feel abandoned by You because sometimes we lose sight of You while we are in the midst of the battles of life.

So today, we have one request. We want to remember how

loving You are, how glorious You are, how strong You are. We're going to take a moment right now to set aside all of our concerns and fears and uncertainties and frustrations and anger.

We want to be like little children who will crawl into Your lap, Daddy God. We want to feel Your arms around us. We're going to allow You to love on us, and we're going to love on You in return, not asking for anything else but this time in Your arms, sheltered beneath the shadow of Your wings.

We know that You are holy. You are worthy. You are the Alpha and Omega, the first and the last. But You have also called us Your children and Your friends. You have shown us Your deep love, Your boundless compassion. And so for this moment, we rest completely in You, like an infant rocked to sleep in his daddy's arms.

Thank You, Lord, that we can rest in You. Thank You for a peace that passes understanding. Thank You.

---

our steps and stops

The steps of a man are established by the Lord, And He delights in his way. When he falls, he will not be hurled headlong, Because the Lord is the One who holds his hand. (Psalm 37:23–24, NASB95)

Heavenly Father, we acknowledge today that our steps are established by You but also our stops. Some of us feel like we have run up against a brick wall in our writing. We believe in our hearts that this is what You have called us to do in this season of our lives and yet every time we turn around there is another roadblock. For some it is no contract. For others it is burnout or writer's block. For still others it is a lack of enjoyment in the process of creating a book.

If these roadblocks are Your stops in our lives, would You

help us to see that and learn to rest in You. Would You help us to be sanctified in the midst of a refining process. Would You grow us up in You and help us to respond with maturity and grace. Would You quiet our fears.

Hold our hands, Lord Jesus. Walk with us through the refining fires. We want to be yoked with You throughout our lives here on earth. Be glorified, O God Most High.

---

story-tellers

All true evangelists originally were and fundamentally remain Story-tellers … Movies are fine, it just tends to take millions of dollars to make really good ones—and lots of really talented people. And those very talented people are then given permission to be the movers and shapers of the worldview we absorb from them through their stories. — Mike Freeman, Pastor, VCF Boise

Father God, we lift up to You the Christian writing community and we ask You to help us write stories with worldviews that will move and shape our world for Christ. Grant us the ability to write truth in such a way that it will draw readers into a closer relationship with You.

Lord, You have called us to run the race, to be down on the playing field, not to sit in the stands and cheer. Give us courage and endurance and wisdom through the power of Your Holy Spirit to write words that will motivate the body of Christ to do exactly that. To pursue You daily. To serve You daily. To worship You daily. Make us true evangelists through the stories You have called us to write.

In Christ's name we pray, Amen

write what we see

Write in a book what you see... (Revelation 1:11a, NASB95)

Father God, You have called us to write. You have given us talent and told us to use it for Your purposes and not our own. We pray that we won't waste the gifts You have bestowed. Grant us courage to write truth and the ability to write with power.

Lord, there are those among us who have experienced and witnessed various trials, trials that You want to use to heal others who are hurting. Would You allow us to speak truth into lives touched by addiction, by infidelity, by prejudice, by cancer, by human trafficking, by deceitfulness, by physical and/or emotional abuse, by depression, by betrayal, by faithlessness, by legalism. Would You help us to take those painful places in our own hearts and write about them, to "write in a book what we see."

Bless us, Father, with an overwhelming abundance of trust and faith in You.

Amen

be present while we write

The Lord your God is in your midst, A victorious warrior. He will exult over you with joy, He will be quiet in His love, He will rejoice over you with shouts of joy. (Zephaniah 3:17, NASB95)

Abba Father, how amazing that You exult over us with joy. How amazing that You are in our midst. Sometimes it is much too much to take in.

Lord, You have made us wordsmiths, men and women who are called to tell stories that reveal truth to the world around us.

But before we can write words worth reading, we must engage with *the* Word. Would You make our highest priority to be our relationship with Jesus. Would You put a hunger and thirst into our hearts so that we cannot be satisfied with less than You want for us.

As we turn to our work today, Father, we ask for words that will bring comfort to those who hurt, that will bring courage to those who fear, that will bring laughter to those who mourn, that will bring rest to those who toil. Holy Spirit, we invite You to come and be present as we write.

In Jesus' holy name, Amen

---

write life

Death and life are in the power of the tongue. (Proverbs 18:21a, NASB95)

Ah, Lord God, You have given words great power on this earth. You spoke the world into existence. You spoke and there was night and day. We ask Your forgiveness for those times when we have misused the power of words, when we have injured rather than healed. We have the power to change someone's life by the words we speak and write.

Today we ask that You would put a guard over our mouths and a guard over our writing instruments. Help us to create stories and to speak truths that will build up and mend a hurting world. Help us to speak and write LIFE.

Amen and Amen

none like you

There is none like You, O Lord; You are great, and great is Your name in might. Who would not fear You, O King of the nations? Indeed it is Your due! For among all the wise men of the nations And in all their kingdoms, There is none like You. (Jeremiah 10:6–7, NASB95)

Our Father in heaven, it is true. There is none like You. Today we declare Your glory. You are King of the nations and our submission is Your due.

You have called us to write for Your kingdom. Whether for one book or a thousand, we commit our minds, our pens, our computers to You. Help us to reach a hurting world with the good news of Jesus Christ, apart from whom there is no salvation. Help us to write clean and true and clear. Don't allow us to fall victim to fear of what others might think. You have called us to write and so help us to write—and then to leave the results of our writing in Your hands. Take our words where they are needed, whether that be one reader or a million readers.

Thank You, Lord, for the wonders of modern technology. Sometimes it can feel more like a curse, it's true, but we also recognize that it has increased our sphere of influence beyond anything we could have dreamed of not all that long ago. Help us to speak boldly into those spheres of influence. Help us to live uprightly and to never bring shame or embarrassment onto the cause of Christ because of our words or actions.

And Holy Spirit, we pray that each person reading this prayer, no matter when that is, would be more aware than ever of Your presence in their lives. Fill them up to overflowing with the joy of the Lord today.

In Jesus' mighty name, Amen

stand in the gap

The LORD also will be a stronghold for the oppressed, A stronghold in times of trouble; And those who know Your name will put their trust in You, For You, O LORD, have not forsaken those who seek You. (Psalm 9:9-10, NASB95)

Father God, these are most assuredly times of trouble for so many. The stock market falling. Wars and rumors of wars. Unemployment. Health problems. The world thrashing around, longing for true leadership and finding no one to stand in the gap. Have mercy, Lord!

We know Your name. Your name is Jesus, the Alpha and the Omega, the First and the Last, the Beginning and the End. Your name is Counselor, Mighty God, Jehovah-Jireh, Ancient of Days. Your name is Living Water, Resurrection and Life, the Good Shepherd, the Judge of All. Your name is Spirit of Truth, our Comforter, our Advocate. Your name is above all names in heaven and on earth.

Here we stand, declaring that we put our trust in You. You have never forsaken those who seek You. We are seeking. Show us how we might be lights in the darkness within our spheres of influence. Give us hearts of mighty warriors. Help us to think less of "me" and more of others. Sharpen our minds, even when we are weary.

No matter what, we will praise You.

---

search our hearts

O Lord, I call upon You; hasten to me! Give ear to my voice when I call to You! May my prayer be counted as incense before You; The lifting up of my hands as the evening offering. Set a guard, O Lord, over my mouth; Keep watch over the door of my lips. Do not incline my heart to any evil thing, To practice deeds of wickedness With men who do iniquity; And do not let me eat of their delicacies. (Psalm 141:1–4, NASB95)

Father God, today we ask that You would search our hearts and know if there be any hurtful way in us. Lead us in Your everlasting way. Help us to trust You when we are confused or scared. We look at the wickedness in the world around us and we cry out for justice on behalf of the weak and afflicted. We see the suffering and we long for bodies that are not subject to disease and the aging process.

Sovereign Lord, You formed us, You purposed us. Wonderful are Your works. You know all of our days and all of our words, both spoken and written. Make them good words, Lord. Words that will lift up and not strike down. Words that will correct wrong thinking (including our own). Words that will encourage instead of defeat. Words that will lighten a heart or bring a tear to an eye.

Today, Lord God, we will meditate on all You're doing. We will muse on the work of Your hands. We will stretch out our hands to You. Our souls long for You, as a parched land. Only You can satisfy.

In the beloved name of Jesus, Amen

---

stand firm

Therefore be careful how you walk, not as unwise men but as wise, making the most of your time, because the days are evil. So then do not be foolish, but understand what the will of the Lord is. (Ephesians 5:15–17, NASB95)

Father God, we acknowledge today that the devil schemes against You and against us. He seeks to make us ineffective in serving You and Your kingdom on earth. Lord, we submit our wills to You. Help us to understand Your will in all things. Help us to don Your full armor so that we may stand firm.

We give You our writing. We would rather not write if it isn't of You. Sift our hearts and remove any impurities found there. Replace them with compassion and love and mercy and grace. Teach us and then let us share with our readers all that You have taught us. Lord, in everything we do and are, help us to submit to Your authority.

Amen

self ... self ... self

An argument started among them as to which of them might be the greatest. (Luke 9:46, NASB95)

Lord God, we come before You today and ask that You would convict us of our desire to be the greatest. We are so like Your twelve disciples, subject to the same jealousies and self-interests. But we want to be more like You, Jesus. We want to set aside self-exaltation, self-will, self-absorption, self-sufficiency, self-protection, self-righteousness, self-indulgence, self ... self ... self ...

Father, today, we lay our writing before You and ask that, even as You bless it to touch the lives of others, You would also use it to change our own hearts, to change our own minds, to turn us toward You. May our words further Your kingdom. May they exalt You and not us.

In the powerful name of Christ we pray, Amen

we will stand

Lord God, today we declare that You are the Master of our lives and the Master of our writing. We continue to try to make sense of this crazy business called publishing, but we acknowledge that only You know the future. So we will do everything we can to be wise and to be prudent, but ultimately what we will finally do is stand. We will stand in Your power. We will stand in Your peace.

For those among us currently struggling with a work-in-progress, would You give us miraculous clarity of thought. Would You unleash unexpected creativity. Would You give us a glimpse of the difference this "problem story" is going to make in the lives of readers. Would You help us understand the part our writing will play in the plan You have for our lives and the lives of our readers.

Lord, help us to submit everything to Your will. Renew in us the joy of our salvation. Restore to us the wonder of what You accomplished by Your death and resurrection.

Amen

bless our fellow writers

A new commandment I give you: Love one another. As I have loved you, so you must love one another. All men will know that you are My disciples if you love one another. (John 13:34, 35, NASB95)

Jesus, we thank You for each and every one of our brothers and sisters in Christ in the writing community. We ask today that You bless them, individually and collectively. We ask that You would pour out fresh inspiration upon these writers. Help the words to flow. Give them excitement over their works-in-progress and a love of the craft of writing that they haven't felt in a while. Remind them that the talent they have was given to them by You. Help them to release it to Your will, to use as You see fit.

Would You protect our hearts today. We can wound so easily. Would You help us to turn our hurts over to You. Help us to be obedient to Your word in all of our ways.

In Your name we pray, Amen

---

an offering of words

But King David said to Ornan, "No, but I will surely buy it for the full price; for I will not take what is yours for the Lord, or offer a burnt offering which costs me nothing." (1 Chronicles 21:24, NASB95)

Lord God, we come to You and offer up the words we have written and the words we will write today and this week and this month and this year. Forgive us for complaining at times about how hard it is to write our books. Help us to be like David, not willing to offer anything to You that costs us nothing. For no matter how hard it is, no matter how much we struggle, it is little in comparison with Your grace and mercy.

Lord, we acknowledge today that You are our Shiloh (peacemaker) and our Scepter and the Rock of our Salvation and the Light of the Morning and the Captain of the Host. Holy God, You are the Lifter Up of our Heads and our Rock and Fortress and our Restorer. You are so much more than we can express. Would You reveal a new attribute of Your character to us this week. Would You help us catch a glimpse of Your beauty and power and might that we have never seen before.

Father, words are a mighty tool. Would You empower our words to show a hurting world who You are and what You want to do in individual lives. Would You expand our territory. Would

You surprise us in the days to come in the way You move on our behalf.

Help us to meet each day with thanksgiving and praise in our hearts, no matter the circumstances of our lives.

Jesus, be glorified. Amen

---

no matter the circumstances

"If it be so, our God whom we serve is able to deliver us from the furnace of blazing fire; and He will deliver us out of your hand, O king. But even if He does not, let it be known to you, O king, that we are not going to serve your gods or worship the golden image that you have set up." (Daniel 3:17–18, NASB95)

Holy God, we pray that we will choose to worship and serve only You. That no matter the circumstances in our lives we would lift our voices in praise to You. You are Holy and Just and Merciful and Loving. You do not give us a stone when we ask for bread. You have poured out Your grace upon us. We love You because You first loved us. Without that love, we would be lost.

Lord, would You cause us to stop today and meditate upon who You are and what You have done for us. Would You fill us with the wonder of a child. Would You give each one of us joy and peace. Would You cause us to rise up and praise You, for if we don't, the very rocks will do so in our place.

Holy Spirit, would You fill our thoughts with the words You want us to write today. Whatever we do today, may it be done for You. Let us never give something to You that costs us nothing. May we give You the first fruits of our money, the first fruits of our time, and the first fruits of our labor.

In the blessed name of Jesus, the Messiah, Amen

god's great army

Finally, be strong in the Lord and in the strength of His might. Put on the full armor of God, so that you will be able to stand firm against the schemes of the devil. (Ephesians 6:10–11, NASB95)

Almighty God, creator of heaven and earth, we come before You today, wanting to don the full armor You have provided to us. We state in faith that we are standing firm against the schemes of the devil, schemes of deceit, schemes of marital trials, schemes of sickness and injury, schemes of financial distress. Whatever the enemy's schemes, we will not be moved. We know that our struggles are truly against powers and forces of darkness in the unseen places. Therefore, we take up the full armor You have provided to us so that we can resist and, having done everything, stand firm.

Today we gird our loins with truth, with Your truth. Burn Your truth into our minds and hearts, O God. We put on the breastplate of Christ's righteousness, for apart from Jesus and His righteousness, our hearts are exposed to the wickedness of this present world. Our feet are tightly shod in the Gospel of Peace, and wherever we go this day, may we spread that good news to others. We have taken up the shield of faith because it enables us to extinguish the flaming arrows that the evil one shoots at us, and we thank You for its provision. Lord, we put on the helmet of salvation which You provided by Your death and resurrection; keep our minds pure beneath it.

O Lord, help us to arm ourselves with the sword of the Spirit which is the word of God. Help us to pray at all times in the Spirit and to be on the alert. Help us to pray for each other. Help us to remember those who cannot speak for themselves. Help us to march forth with courage into this troubled world.

Today, we put the cross of Christ before us, and we march out, members of Your great army, an army both strong and filled with compassion.

Blessed be the name of the Lord! Amen

---

all we need

The Lord is my strength and song, And He has become my salvation; This is my God, and I will praise Him; My father's God, and I will extol Him. (Exodus 15:2, NASB95)

Jehovah-Jireh, we acknowledge today that You provide us with all that we need. You even supplied the sacrifice for our sins so that we might escape Your judgement. Holy God, Your salvation comes only through Your Son, and we do humbly confess today our dependence upon Him.

For those of us who have sickness in our bodies or in the body of someone we love, would You send healing, whether through a divine touch or through the touch of a doctor's hands.

For those of us who are struggling to get our stories written, would You stir up the gift that is in us. Would You remind us that You prepared the work beforehand for us to walk in. You knew the stories we would write even before we were born because You are the Creator of all things.

For those of us who need to be drawn into a closer relationship with Jesus, would You place a hunger in our hearts that will be satisfied by nothing less than time in Your holy presence. Help us to be still and know that You are God.

more! more! more!

And my God will supply all your needs according to His riches in glory in Christ Jesus. (Philippians 4:19, NASB95)

Father God, we come before You today to declare that You, our God, *always* supply for Your children's needs. And so very often, You do so in miraculous, surprising ways. What joy we feel when we catch these glimpses of Your love for us. What amazement is ours when You shower that love and Your blessings all over us. Some days we feel as if we are drowning in Your love. What a way to go!!!

We are greedy for more of You, Jesus. More! More! More!

Lord, help us not make the mistake of despising the mountaintop experiences we have known just because they don't happen all the time. And don't let us make the mistake of chasing after the mountaintop experiences and forgetting that the valleys are where we find ourselves most often. Help us to remember the mountaintops where You give us glimpses of Your glory, for it is the memories of Your glory that give us strength to walk out our lives here on earth.

Father, we pray that You will meet the needs of Christian writers today. Needs for physical healing. Needs for emotional healing. Needs for financial resources. Needs for the knowledge of where we should go and what we should do to serve You. And Lord, as You did for Paul, would You teach us to be content in whatever state we find ourselves, whether we have much or we have little. One place You never mean for us to have little is in the area of joy. You mean for us to have that in abundance. Would You multiply joy in our lives today.

In the precious name of Jesus, Amen

jesus is the root

For the Lord your God is a compassionate God; He will not fail you nor destroy you nor forget the covenant with your fathers which He swore to them. (Deuteronomy 4:31, NASB95)

Father God, You have shown us great compassion. Again and again in our lives, You have showered us with mercy. We acknowledge that You are the beginning and the end. Jesus, you have sent Your angel to testify to Your church that You are the root and the descendant of David, the bright morning star. Let those of us who hear say, "Come."

Lord, You know our needs. You see who is sick. You see who is weary. You see who is in need. But You do more than see us. You draw near. And so today we press into You. As little children, we cry, "Abba. Father. Daddy!" You will not give us a stone when we ask for bread.

You have asked us to stand in faith, and so that's what we will do today. We will put on the full armor of God and stand. We trust You, Lord, to do what is best for us and for Your kingdom. We want our lives to be a testimony to Your glory.

Amen

---

show us your glory

Today, Lord, we want to testify to the truth of Your word.

Along with Moses, we say, "I pray You, show me Your glory!" Let our presence be with Your presence. Let our hearts be overwhelmed by Your love.

Along with Moses, we pray, "O Lord, I pray, let the Lord go along in our midst, even though the people are so obstinate, and pardon our iniquity and our sin, and take us as Your own possession." Forgive us our sins of pride and self-sufficiency. Forgive us for our jealousy and envy. Walk among us, despite our obstinacy. Because of the sacrifice of Your Son, we are Your people and we want You with us, every moment of every hour.

Father God, just as You filled Bezalel, the son of Uri, the son of Hur, of the tribe of Judah, with Your Spirit, just as You filled him in wisdom, in understanding and in knowledge and in all craftsmanship as he followed your designs for the tabernacle, would You do the same for us in regard to our writing so that our work would glorify You.

And Lord, would You make these words in Isaiah ring loudly in our hearts today, reminding us where we can run for help:

Do you not know? Have you not heard?
The Everlasting God, the Lord, the Creator of the ends of the earth
Does not become weary or tired.
His understanding is inscrutable.
He gives strength to the weary,
And to him who lacks might He increases power.
Though youths grow weary and tired,
And vigorous young men stumble badly,
Yet those who wait for the Lord
Will gain new strength;
They will mount up with wings like eagles,
They will run and not get tired,
They will walk and not become weary.

Make us mount up with wings like eagles today, Father God. Help us soar.

In the name of the King of kings and Lord of lords, Amen

he knows us

O Lord, our Lord, how majestic is Your name in all the earth!

Father God, today we want to sing Your praises. We want to shout Your glory to the mountaintops and to the deepest parts of the sea. You are a God of miracles who is intimately involved in our lives. You know our thoughts. You know our names. How amazing!

Holy Spirit, blessed Comforter, there are those among us who are bone weary, whose emotions are laid bare, who barely have the energy to read this prayer, let alone to write for You. Would You touch us right now. Would You remind us that the joy of the Lord is our strength. That You have come with power and with might to help us in our hour of need. Would You refresh us today. And above all, would You help us to lay our burdens—those family problems that have consumed us, those financial problems that awaken us in the middle of the night, those physical problems that threaten to overwhelm us—at the feet of Jesus. Would You help us lay it ALL down and not take it back up again.

Amen and Amen. Blessed be the name of the Lord.

hear our supplication

A man of too many friends comes to ruin, But there is a friend who sticks closer than a brother. (Proverbs 18:24, NASB95)

Jesus, blessed Redeemer! How amazing that You have called those who trust in You "friends." You were there at the beginning of time. You spoke the world into existence. Who are we that You should think of us? And yet You do. You think of us and know us by name and collect our tears. Our names are written in the Book of Life.

No matter what trials we face today, we acknowledge that we can take it to You in prayer, for You stick closer to us than a brother. We proclaim, like the psalmist, *"The LORD has heard my supplication, The LORD receives my prayer."*

Grant us, Jesus, a life worthy of Your calling. Draw us closer to You throughout this day, this week, this year. May the words of our mouths and the meditations of our hearts be acceptable in Your sight, O Lord, our Strength and our Redeemer.

upheld by his right hand

I have sunk in deep mire, and there is no foothold; I have come into deep waters, and a flood overflows me. I am weary with my crying; my throat is parched; My eyes fail while I wait for my God. (Psalm 69:2–3, NASB95)

Father God, today we want to pray specifically for those writers who feel like the above verses about their writing careers. In this crazy economy, with the business of publishing changing faster than we can comprehend, sometimes we feel as if we are without a foothold and the deep waters of a flood are rushing over our heads. We're weary and parched and blind. We've run out of ourselves—we are completely empty—while we wait for You. Some of us are without contracts. Others among us are horribly late with a book and feel as if our creativity has shriveled within us into nothing.

Help!

"O God, You are my God; I shall seek You earnestly; My soul thirsts for You, my flesh yearns for You, In a dry and weary land where there is

no water. Thus I have seen You in the sanctuary, To see Your power and Your glory. Because Your lovingkindness is better than life, My lips will praise You. So I will bless You as long as I live; I will lift up my hands in Your name. My soul is satisfied as with marrow and fatness, And my mouth offers praises with joyful lips. When I remember You on my bed, I meditate on You in the night watches, For You have been my help, And in the shadow of Your wings I sing for joy. My soul clings to You; Your right hand upholds me. " (Psalm 63:1–8, NASB95)

Yes, Lord! We will offer praises to You with joyful lips. Despite our circumstances, we will lift up our hands in praise to You. Our souls are satisfied. We fall to our knees at the foot of the cross and we cling to You. Your right hand upholds us. Every single one of us.

And so we rest and find peace because we know that You will never leave or forsake us.

In Your beautiful name, Amen

jesus, our song

Then you will say on that day, "I will give thanks to You, O LORD; For although You were angry with me, Your anger is turned away, And You comfort me. Behold, God is my salvation, I will trust and not be afraid; For the LORD GOD is my strength and song, And He has become my salvation." (Isaiah 12:1-2, NASB95)

Father God, we come to you today on behalf of the Christians in the writing community, and we ask that You pour out Your anointing upon the books that we write. And as we write our stories, Lord, would You remind us afresh of all the blessings You have given us so generously. We thank You that Your deserved wrath and anger fell upon Jesus in our stead. We are so thankful for Your mercy and grace. We will trust in You and not be afraid of what today or tomorrow or next week or next month or next year will bring with it.

Jesus, You are our strength and our song. Would You let that song well up in our hearts today and spill over upon those around us. Would you embolden us to share You with a down-trodden and discouraged world.

And Lord, for those of us who find ourselves staring at a deadline that will arrive all too soon, would You multiply our efforts and our words, granting us a renewed enthusiasm for our projects and divine inspiration.

We thank You, Lord, for this day because it is the day that You have made. We will rejoice and be glad in it.

Amen

covenants and testimonies

Make me know Your ways, O Lord; Teach me Your paths. (Psalm 25:4, NASB95)

Heavenly Father, we want to crawl into Your lap today and let You hold us. Some days, that is all we need, to sit and to be in Your presence. All the paths of the Lord are lovingkindness and truth to those who keep His covenant and His testimonies. We want to be the children who keep those covenants and testimonies.

Would You remind us today that everything we do should be done unto You. Would You make us ever aware of Your holiness and Your grace. Would You draw our attention off of our careers, our budgets, our worries and remind us that You are the God of our salvation, that our lives, our very breaths belong to You.

Would you keep us from looking at other writers and comparing our work, our contracts, our marketing, our PR to theirs. What is the career (or the reviews or the praises) of another writer to us? If You want someone else to have all of that, it isn't our concern. We must follow You. We *will* follow You. Pleasing You is all that matters.

O Lord God, may we be faithful. You have prepared good works for us to walk in. May we walk in them.

In Christ's glorious name we pray, Amen

upon this truth

It is the Lord of hosts whom you should regard as holy. And He shall be your fear, And He shall be your dread. (Isaiah 8:13, NASB95)

Most holy, most awesome God, it is You alone whom we fear. It is You alone who is able to move the mountains. It is You alone who is able to calm the storm. Those who don't know you say, "It is a conspiracy!" and they fear it and dread it. But we who are called Your people fear and dread only You. We stand in awe of You, and we bow down in worship to You.

There are storms raging around some of us today. There are mountains standing in our way today. But Lord, we will not fear the storm or dread the mountains. We will lift our eyes to see Jesus, the Holy One of Israel, and we declare our faith and trust in You. Upon this truth we stand. We will not be moved.

Amen and Amen

send us!

Then I heard the voice of the Lord, saying, "Whom shall I send, and who will go for Us?" Then I said, "Here am I. Send me!" (Isaiah 6:8, NASB95)

Most Holy God, we have heard Your voice, calling us to serve You, sending us into a world where few will hear as we share about Your mighty deeds, about Your great mercy and abounding grace. And yet we say again, "Here am I. Send me!"

Would You anoint the words that we write this week, infusing them with Your power, Your truths, Your love. Would You allow us to be the body of Christ in miraculous ways to those we meet in person and to those who will read our written words. Father, please don't let us ever be satisfied to sit on the river bank, watching the water sweeping by. Give us the courage to go into that river of the faith life, not just ankle deep, not just waist deep, but all the way up to our necks. Restore to us the joy of our salvation and renew us with right spirits.

Jesus, we say it with unabashed joy. We love You! And we want that love to manifest itself in the way we love others. Here we are, Jesus. Send us!

In Your mighty name we pray, Amen

it takes a lot of compost

Almighty God, Who was and is and is to come. We come to You today, bowing down before Your throne.

In the parable of the wheat and the tares, Your word tells us that the weeds will be taken out and burned at the harvest, not before. But sometimes it's hard for the wheat, Your body of believers, to see above the weeds growing around us. We feel confused and far from You at such times, especially since we cannot see what's happening below the surface.

Would You remind us, Lord, of the work You are doing in the soil at such times. Would You remind us that it takes a lot of compost—trials and tribulation—to make the soil of our hearts able to produce a bountiful harvest for Your glory.

We want our roots to go deeper and deeper so that we might live in true Christian maturity. And as our roots go deeper, would You help our impact upon this world to go wider and wider.

Might we humbly say, when You show us the work You want us to do, "Lord, I can't, but You can." Might we respond, "Yes, Lord. Not my will but Yours be done!"

build the house

Unless the Lord builds the house, they labor in vain who build it.
(Psalm 127:1, NASB95)

Almighty God, You have given us many different gifts, but one gift we share is the gift of writing. We want to use it for Your glory. We want to write stories that will lift and encourage those who read them. We want readers to see You in the pages. We want them to close the book and find themselves several steps closer to You.

But Lord, unless You build the house, we labor in vain. So today we ask You to build the houses of our careers. Jesus, build the house that is our work-in-progress. Not only that, but please build the houses of our marriages, the houses of our relationships with parents, children, grandchildren, the houses of our friendships.

As we open our writing today, we thank You that we can lean in to You and trust in all of Your provisions for us. Blessed be the name of the Lord.

a people of prayer

The magnificence of all true prayer—its nobility, its royalty, its absolute divinity—all stand in this: that it is the greatest act and office that man or angel can ever enter on or perform. Earth is at its very best, and heaven is at its highest, when men and angels magnify their duty of prayer and of praise before the throne of God. The magnificence of God is the source and the measure of the magnificence of prayer. —
Alexander Whyte

Father God, prayer is the highest calling for man. Nothing else we can do surpasses it. You want us to spend time in Your magnificent presence. So Lord, today we ask that above all else, we would be a people of prayer, that we would desire to come away with You and sit at Your feet and listen to Your voice. That we would be hungry for more of You. Jesus, You are magnificent! The light of Your glory causes everything else in our lives to grow small and dim by comparison—our successes and our failures, our worries, our trials, everything.

Father, we humble ourselves before You and trust You with our lives. May it be as You will.

spiritually fit for service

Lord, make us fit for Your service. You've called your children to be Your soldiers here on earth. Having good physical health is important for us all. So is being mentally fit. But if we aren't spiritually fit, we'll find ourselves doing KP duty instead of being in the thick of the battle against the evil of this world. We want to be right on the front lines. We want to do our part to defeat the plans of the enemy and to be fit enough to still swing our swords when the time comes for You to call us home.

And so Father, we ask that You would help us to obtain and maintain good spiritual health. Give us a hunger for Your Word, both the Living Word and the written Word. Help us to make eating of the bread of life the first and most important task of our days. Don't allow us to be satisfied with the food the world has to offer us in a million ways. Fill us up with You, Lord, so that we can offer the world—in our writing and with our lives—what it is starving for, although it may not know it.

Jesus, we want to be a vital part of Your army, the army that brings good news to the afflicted, that binds up the broken-hearted, that proclaims liberty to captives and freedom to prisoners, that comforts those who mourn, and that gives garland instead of ashes, the oil of gladness instead of mourning, and the mantle of praise instead of a spirit of fainting. We want to be among the people who will be called oaks of righteousness, the planting of the Lord, that You may be glorified. (Isaiah 61:1-3)

In Your mighty name we pray, Amen

publish his glorious deeds

Let the whole earth sing to the LORD! Each day proclaim the good news that he saves. Publish his glorious deeds among the nations. Tell everyone about the amazing things he does. Great is the LORD! He is most worthy of praise! (1 Chronicles 16:23-25a, NLT)

What an awesome, amazing, thrilling, unnerving thing it is to be called to publish Your glorious deeds among the nations! Thank You for entrusting it to us.

Would You help us today to find the words to accomplish this task. Would You help us to write true and strong. Would You give us courage to go where others have been afraid to go in order to glorify Your name and proclaim Your good news.

Lord God, we ask for a special pouring out of Your spirit upon the writers of Christian fiction. Whether we are answering a letter to a reader or writing a new scene in a novel, would You infuse our "pens" with Your wisdom, Your power, Your love, Your compassion, Your truth.

And above all else, Jesus, may we be Your hands and feet upon the earth until we join You in paradise or see Your Second Coming in all Your glory.

In His name, Amen

his holiness remains

What an awesome God we serve!

Lord, we join with the angels around Your throne today and cry, "Holy! Holy! Holy!" You are worthy of all our praises. You love us so much, and no matter the circumstances we find ourselves in today, You never change. Your love remains. Your holiness remains. Your mighty power remains.

Father God, we ask today for a mighty outpouring of Your Holy Spirit. Would You anoint the words we write today. Would You anoint the words we speak today. Would You cause us to be Jesus-focused in all that we do, whether we are with our families or all alone, whether we are doing something visible to the world or we are mopping the floor in solitude.

Lord, make us grateful for all that we have. We have much to be grateful for. Break our hearts for the things in this world that break Your heart. Help us to live as You have called us to live. Don't let us settle for less than the miraculous life You preordained for those who follow Christ.

In the mighty name of Jesus we pray, Amen

nothing we desire more

Whom have I in heaven but You? And besides You, I desire nothing on earth. My flesh and my heart may fail, But God is the strength of my heart and my portion forever. (Psalm 73:25-26, NASB95)

Adonai, we praise You today. You are the source of our lives. Apart from You, we have no good thing. There is nothing we desire on this earth more than we desire You.

We thank You, Father, for the many good things, the many blessings, that You have poured out upon us. Even as we read the words of this prayer, we pause to thank You for those we love, for our work, for our homes, for Your presence in our lives. Our voices rise in thanksgiving. Let our very lives be like a love song to You. May worship permeate every waking moment of this day, of this week, of this month, of this year. May we exalt You with our voices, with our actions, with our service to others.

Father, we confess that we don't always keep the cross before us. Help us to do so today. Be first in our lives. If we don't love You enough, overwhelm us with Your love. Help us to know, deep down in our hearts, that there is nothing we can do or not do to make You love us more or to love us less.

Jesus, You are our Sovereign Lord, and we praise and worship You this day.

deep and wide

Lord God, You are our hiding place and our shield. We wait for Your word.

Abba Father, our world is so troubled. Sometimes it's hard not to despair over the things we read and the things we see. We know there is trouble everywhere, but today, we especially pray for the nations where Christian writers live. We may not know them all, but You do. Lord, we pray for revival in these countries. We pray that Your truth would rise above the culture and be recognized for what it is and Who it's from. We pray for another move of Your Holy Spirit around the globe.

God, cause that revival to begin in us, in the hearts of those who call You LORD. Help us to put aside the wrong thinking that so easily takes up residence in our minds and hearts because of our culture. Holy Spirit, rain down on us. Change us and mold us. You are the Potter, we are the clay. Do with us what You will. Take us deep—in prayer, in Your word, in fellowship with the saints—so that we might go wide—in acts of compassion, in writing stories that glorify You and encourage Your people.

Adonai, we worship You. We fall down before You in adoration. We put You on the throne and ask that in all things concerning us, Your will be done.

For Your glory and our joy, Amen

to love mercy

Father God, Your word tells us that You have shown us what is good and You have told us what You require of us: *To act justly and to love mercy and to walk humbly with You, our God* (Micah 6:8). Today, would You help us to live this way.

Would You teach us to be fair in all of our dealings with others. Would You put a watch over our tongues when we get frustrated with a family member or when talking to a customer service rep over the telephone. Would you help us to rise up and resist injustice to others, to the poor and the downtrodden. Place concern in our hearts for all social injustice. Remind us that You have called us to a life of service as soldiers in Your army.

Lord, would You put Your compassion into our hearts. Help us to shower grace onto the people around us, first to members of our families, then to our friends and others in the workplace, and finally to strangers. Break our hearts, Lord, for the things that break Your heart. Help us to think of others first and ourselves second.

Abba God, grant us true humility. Would You stifle our selfish natures and subdue our natural pride and our inclination to have things our own way. Cause us to see the cross before us, to act as Jesus did when He walked this earth. Help us to set aside our old natures as an act of will and to put on the new nature that is guided by the fruit of Your Holy Spirit.

Today, Lord, let us begin to truly act justly, to love mercy, and to walk humbly with You.

In Christ's name we pray, Amen

blessed be his name

Adonai, Master of the universe, Lord of our hearts—

To You, we lift up our souls. We put our trust in You, no matter the circumstances that surround us today. Show us Your ways, O Lord, and teach us Your path. You are the God of our salvation. Remember, O Lord, Your compassion and love, for they are from everlasting.

Remember not the sins of our youths and our transgressions; remember us according to Your love and for the sake of Your goodness, O Lord.

Gracious and upright are You, Lord; therefore You teach sinners in Your way. You guide the humble in doing right and teach Your ways to the lowly. All of Your paths are love and faithfulness to those who keep Your covenant and Your testimonies.

Our eyes are ever looking to You, Jesus, for You have plucked our feet out of the net, and we know You shall continue to pluck our feet out of the net.

We surrender every concern, worry, fear, illness, and heartbreak unto You today. Blessed be the Name of the Lord!

---

glorious grace

Abba Father, how great and mighty You are. Thank You for all the love and blessings You have lavished upon us. You have blessed us with every spiritual blessing in the heavenly realms because we are united with Christ. Before the beginning of the world, You loved us and chose us in Christ. You decided in advance, even knowing all that we would be, to adopt us into Your family. We praise You, Lord, for the glorious grace You've poured out on we who belong to Your dear Son.

Thank You for revealing to us Your mysterious plan regarding Jesus. At the right time, He will bring everything together under His authority.

Now Lord, we thank You for the writers of Christian literature, for our brothers and sisters in Christ who seek to serve You with our lives and with our writing. We ask You, glorious Father, to give each one of us spiritual wisdom and insight so that we might grow in our knowledge of You. We pray that our hearts will be flooded with light so that we can understand the confident hope You have given to those You called—Your holy people. We also pray that we will understand the incredible greatness of God's power for those who believe in Jesus.

Adonai, we give You this day, this week, our lives, the very breaths we breathe. Do with us as You will.

In the mighty name of Jesus we pray, Amen

his grace is amazing

Lord, today we don't want to ask for anything but to experience Your wonderful presence. We want to seek You, to find You, to love You. And we thank You for the many Christian song writers who give us words and melodies to help express what is in our hearts.

We love You, Lord Jesus. We are overwhelmed by the love You pour out on us. We are so grateful that You call us to sit at Your feet and dwell in Your presence. Your grace is amazing, and You leave us breathless today. Holy, holy, holy is the Lamb of God.

Hallelujah! and Amen

---

finished correctly

Be strong and courageous, and do the work. Don't be afraid or discouraged, for the Lord God, my God, is with you. He will not fail you or forsake you. He will see to it that all the work ... is finished correctly. (1 Chronicles 28:20, NLT)

Lord, You have called us to write for Your glory. You put us with our particular publishers/editors/agents/critique partners at this particular time and for a particular reason. But there are times we just want to throw up our hands and quit. We need to write so many words every day to make our deadlines, but the stories in our heads feel like they're going nowhere. We're discouraged and stymied.

Lift our discouragement today. Make us strong and courageous and help us to do the work.

We thank You for choosing us to be Your scribes on earth in our generation. While we have earthly contracts and/or earthly employers, You Lord, are our ultimate publisher, editor, boss. Help us to work for You with enthusiasm and joy.

Jesus, defeat those people and circumstances that seek to defeat us. Help us to do our part so You can do Your part. Grant us perseverance and tenacity. Surprise us with an abundance of ideas. Give us strong bodies that won't hurt as we put in the hours required at our computers. Close us off from unnecessary distractions. Please, Lord, see to it that all the work regarding our works-in-progress is finished correctly.

Amen

---

his written words matter

Father God, eternal and holy, You spoke words and the universe was created. King Jesus, You are the Living Word.

Words matter.

Today, would You give us a love for Your written word so that we in turn can write words that will make a difference to those who read them. Apart from Your word, we cannot know truth. If we don't eat the bread of Your truth, we cannot grow strong. Make us strong, Lord. Fill us up with audacious faith this day. Help us to make You, the invisible God, visible to those around us.

In the name of Christ we ask it, Amen

prayer for the new year

. . .

the bread that satisfies

Abba, here we are in the new year. A clean slate for us to write upon with our lives.

Help us to write upon this year in ways that will glorify You. Make this a year when we step into the deep waters of the things of Your Kingdom. Let us throw off everything that hinders us from running Your race, from living full-out for You. Jesus, don't allow us to be satisfied with the status quo. Make us courageous members of Your army.

We pray particularly for the new stories that will be written in the months to come. Father, would You cause us to stop and pray before we write—and then to listen to Your answers. Would You give us stories that will proclaim Your greatness, Your wisdom, Your love to a world that is lost and hurting. Would You help us to write words that will encourage our brothers and sisters in the church. Lord, we live in perilous times. Don't allow us to withdraw because of the dangers. Help us to move forward with brave hearts.

And Father, stir up a new passion for Your written word in

our spirits. Make us hungry for it daily. You are the bread that satisfies.

In Christ's name, Amen

---

lord, you are timeless

Father God, another year has ended. It passed in the blink of an eye. Sometimes it feels as if our lives are disappearing before we can actually live them.

But You, Lord, are timeless, and You created Your image-bearers to live for eternity. We are so thankful that You sent Your Son to earth in order to provide a bridge over the sin-gap so that we might spend eternity with You. Better is one day in Your court than a thousand elsewhere.

As we turn the calendar to the new year, help us to put Your name and our relationship with You at the very top of our goal setting and to-do lists. You know what triumphs and trials await us, but we do not. We ask that You would keep trials from our path, but if they should come, we ask for the strength and the wisdom and the faith to walk through them in a way that brings You glory and in a way that makes us a little more Christlike.

For Thine is the Kingdom and the Power and the Glory forever. Amen

---

great treasure

"The kingdom of heaven is like a treasure hidden in the field, which a man found and hid again; and from joy over it he goes and sells everything that he has, and buys that field." (Matthew 13:44, NASB2020)

Lord Jesus, we acknowledge as the new year begins that the kingdom of heaven is a great treasure for those who trust and follow You. Your kingdom is here now but is still to come, and it is worth everything we have and everything we are to obtain it.

And Jesus, we acknowledge that we, Your children, are Your treasure. You sought us. You bought us. And we thank You for all that You paid to redeem us and make us the children of God.

We further acknowledge that You didn't bestow treasures upon us so that we would keep them to ourselves. Make us a generous people, Lord, with Your riches, with Your wisdom, with Your glory. Help us to share with the world around us through our words, both in writing and in speaking. Open our hearts. Make us wise and careful. Help us to be clear speaking and clear thinking.

Jesus, we love You. We worship and adore You. Cause this to be a year of renewal and revival, first in your church and then in the world in which we live.

In Your mighty name we pray, Amen

first and foremost

Father God, it's a new year. New calendars hang on our walls and sit on our desks, full of white spaces where we will fill in all those appointments and tasks that represent the busyness of our lives. Help us, Jesus, to enter Your name first each day. Help us to come away with You, to the mountains, to the sea, to a time of solitude and fellowship.

We are writers. We love words. Lord, teach us to love Your word first and foremost. Give us this day our daily bread, for without the sustenance of the Scriptures, without Your voice in our hearts, we cannot live. We can only survive. Help us to drink daily from Your river of life. Make us doers of Your word, not hearers only.

Lord, this world is in trouble. All around us is chaos. Governments crumble. Debt climbs. We sometimes fall into worry about the lives our children or grandchildren or other loved ones will inherit should You tarry. Help us to keep our eyes on You, Jesus, the author and perfecter of our faith. Help us cast off fear and put on trust. For we know our Redeemer lives.

Amen

we need a vision

Where there is no vision, the people are unrestrained, But happy is he who keeps the law. (Proverbs 29:18, NASB95)

Father God, as writers, we need a vision. We need *Your* vision.

Like St. Francis before us, we want the books we write to be instruments of Your peace. We want to sow love where there is hate, to give hope where there is despair, to share joy in place of sadness.

Give us twenty-twenty vision. Open our eyes and our hearts in this new year to write amazing stories that reflect Your glory.

We ask it in Your blessed name, Amen

all things new!

O Lord God, You have made all things new!!

There is something about a new year, a fresh calendar, that gives us a sense of hope, that lets us dream of doing more things right than we do wrong. Father, help us to lean into You this year. Help us to trust You with the hard places as well as the easy places. Help us to trust You when our health is bad or when we face a financial crisis. Help us to credit You for every one of our blessings. Help us to be a people of praise no matter our mood or circumstances. Help us to show joy to a world that is critical and negative. Help us to be a generous people, giving far more than expected. Help us to love the unlovable.

Jesus, be Thou our vision throughout this year.

We humbly ask it in Your name, Amen

---

a blank page

Father, it's another new year. A clean calendar. A blank page. Help us to be lights on a hill, with our words and our lives. Help us throughout the year to write words that will please You most of all.

In Genesis 3:12, Adam told You that he ate the apple because the woman gave it to him. So almost from the very start, mankind has been placing the blame for our sinful choices on someone else. The joke of the 1970s was, the devil made me do it. Only it's no joke.

Make us different this year, Lord. Help us to promote peace while speaking truth. Convict us of our own sins, of our tendencies to justify and blame others. Draw us closer to Jesus so that we might then reflect Him to others. We live in a troubled, troubled world. Divisions abound. Give each one of us the strength and wisdom and kindness to lessen those divides.

Amen and Amen

another second chance

Almighty God, it's another new year, a time when we look forward and hope for things not yet realized. A fresh beginning. Another second chance.

This year, Lord, create in each one of us a clean heart and renew steadfast spirits within us.

This year, Lord, search us, try us, and see if there be any hurtful way in us and lead us in the everlasting way.

This year, Lord, help us to live by the Spirit and walk by the Spirit.

This year, Lord, let us know Your ways that we may know You, so that we may find favor in Your sight.

This year, Lord, may we be able to comprehend with all the saints what is the breadth and length and height and depth, and may we know the love of Christ which surpasses knowledge, that we may be filled up to all the fullness of God.

Thank You, Jesus.

prayer for mlk day

. . .

true reconciliation

Father God, today is Martin Luther King Jr. Day here in America, and we come to You in prayer, asking for true racial reconciliation to spread across this land. We thank You for the people, past and present, who have worked or now work to bring people of different creeds or race together in unity and understanding.

Lord, would You also work in each one of us to be united as the body of Christ. Your word says that the world will know Christians by our love for one another. Would You fill us to overflowing with love for our brothers and sisters in Christ. May we be known for the love, grace, and mercy we extend to those around us. Forgive us for when we fail to love as we ought. Change our hearts. Make us a people who reach out, seeking to heal rather than harm.

Bless the words we will write this week. Make them be words from Your heart, Sovereign Lord, rather than words from our limited human understanding.

In Jesus' name we ask it, Amen

prayer for valentine's day

. . .

the greatest love

It's February, Lord. The month for lovers, red hearts, candy in abundance, beautiful bouquets, romantic dinners, movies that make us cry. All well and good.

But Jesus, would You help us to remember that You represent the greatest love story ever told. Would You remind us that we are the bride and You are the bridegroom. Help us to be certain that we have oil for our lamps and to be in complete readiness, anticipating Your arrival. It is easy to grow sleepy while we wait. Wake us up, Lord!!

Help us to speak and write the words You have appointed for us to speak and write. Ecclesiastes tells us that the writing of many books is endless, and we know that there are thousands upon thousands of useless books written every year. Don't let ours be counted among them. Help us to write stories that will lift a burden, cheer a heart, encourage a soul, and most of all, help the reader take one step closer to You.

In Jesus' beautiful name we pray, Amen

prayer for presidents' day

. . .

surrendered hearts

Almighty God, Creator of heaven and earth, we come to You today on bended knee and with hearts surrendered to You and Your sovereign will. You have told us in Your word to pray for kings and those in authority. In America on the third Monday in February, we recognize Presidents' Day, a day to honor all those who have led and who currently lead this great nation.

Father, we thank You for the sacrifices of past presidents, for the way You shaped this nation, that despite those who want to rewrite or ignore history, the United States of America was built on godly principles. Lord, Your children sometimes feel like a remnant in this country, but because we have stored Your word in our hearts, we know what amazing things You are able to do with a remnant. Help us to stand in the gap for our country today.

And Lord, we lift up our sitting president to You. We pray for protection. Keep our president safe from anyone who would want to do physical harm. We pray for protection for the family as well. We ask that the president would govern with Your wisdom rather than leaning upon human wisdom. Deliver the president from the curse of pride, a condition that can so easily entangle someone in a position of power. Lord, would You place wise and righteous advisers into the president's inner circle and would You flood Washington DC with a spirit of reconciliation. Finally, Lord, may we be a light to the world in both word and deed.

Father, we ask today that we would use the written word with care. May our labor of writing exalt and honor You.

Amen

prayer for resurrection day

. . .

be glorified

Lord Jesus, thank You for the freedom we enjoy to gather with other believers to celebrate Your resurrection. What joy there is in knowing that You paid the full price for our sins, and that we are promised eternity with You.

Jesus, You told us to ask and said it would be given to us, to seek and we would find, to knock and the door would be opened.

Today we ask for healing for those among us who are ill or in pain. There are many among us who have loved ones who are seriously ill, and so we lift them before Your throne as well, and we ask for You to work miracles as only You can.

Today we ask for success in our writing. Would You put new thoughts into our minds. Would You inspire us to reach higher, to try harder, to do better as we write for Your glory.

Lord, there are times when we are in prayer or in worship and we know that You are *everything*, that You are the only thing we need to be happy or content or satisfied or at peace. And then life comes rushing in, and that knowledge, that feeling, slips away from us. We seek that happiness and contentment and satisfaction and peace in other places or with other people, even when we know it can't be found there. Would You draw us back to You today. Would You refresh us and renew us.

Be glorified, Holy Savior, Precious Friend. Be glorified today.

acceptable words

Jesus our Savior, in this Holy Season, when we celebrate all that You accomplished for us on the cross and through Your resurrection, remind us again of all the reasons we needed and still need a Savior. We acknowledge today that we don't just need rescued from the sin that so easily entangles us, but we also need rescued from thinking we can save ourselves through our law-keeping, by perfectionism. Help us to be obedient to Your will, but save us from thinking that it will cause You to love us more or better. If our hearts have grown cold, Lord, stir afresh that fire of love we felt toward You in the hour we first believed.

May the words of our mouths and the words that we write, be acceptable in Your sight, O Lord, our rock and our Redeemer.

And everyone says, Amen

jesus, the answer

Lord Jesus, Easter represents the hope we have because of what You accomplished on the cross and by Your resurrection.

So many in this world think Christianity is just another religion. Help us to be examples to those around us and to those who read our books so that they might see religion isn't the answer. Only You are the answer. Only You can save. Only You give eternal life.

Today we ask that You would infuse our written words with

the hope You have poured out. Help us to remember that words make a difference. Let us write words that will build up and not tear down. You have given each one of us a calling and a gift or gifts. Help us to use them all for Your glory.

In Your mighty name we pray, Amen

---

christ laid it down

Holy, Holy, Holy
Is the LORD God Almighty
Who was
And is
And is to come!

Jesus, two thousand years ago, You chose to step down out of heaven and to write Yourself into the story of history and into the stories of our lives. You came as a baby. You walked this earth. You healed the sick and You raised the dead. And then, when the proper time arrived, You voluntarily laid down Your life to pay for our sins.

Lord, make us truly thankful for the grace and mercy You showed to all mankind, and particularly to each one of us who have chosen to say "Yes!" to You.

As we walk through Passion Week, would You make us mindful of those who do not know the part You want to play in their stories. Would You remind us to pray for them, and would You remind us to share with them. Would you embolden our words, both written and spoken, and would You soften our hearts. Make Your words become a part of us.

This week, we remember You in Your last communion, we remember the stripes You bore on Your back, and we remember Your crucifixion. And most important of all, we remember Your resurrection and what it has meant in the world down through time.

Jesus, You are the First and the Last
The Beginning and the End
The Alpha and Omega
The King of kings
And the Lord of lords.

Forever and Always, Amen

prayer for memorial day

. . .

how majestic is your name

O Lord, our Lord, How majestic is Your name in all the earth, Who have displayed Your splendor above the heavens! (Psalm 8:1, NASB95)

Father God, on this Memorial Day, we pause in our activities to lift words of thanksgiving to You.

We thank You for the freedom we enjoy. Help us never to take it for granted.

We thank You for the privilege of being able to own and read the Bible. Help us never to abuse that privilege by neglecting to meet with You in Your word.

We thank You for the abundance of grace You have poured out upon America. Now we ask that You pour out revival and let it begin with each one of us.

We thank You for the gift of family and friends. Help us to love as You have called us to love.

In the blessed name of Jesus we pray, Amen

prayer for independence day

. . .

true freedom

If my people who are called by my name will humble themselves and pray and seek my face and turn from their wicked ways, I will hear from heaven and will forgive their sins and restore their land. (2 Chronicles 7:14, NLT)

Father God, as we in America celebrate the 4th of July, our Independence Day, would you remind us of our desperate need for You. Remind us that true freedom is found only in You. Help us to walk in Your ways daily, hourly, minute by minute. As a nation, we have wandered far from You. Call men and women of integrity into service in our country, and help Your church, Your people, to lead the way in righteousness, in compassion, in humility. Help us to be the men and women of God that we were born again to be.

For Your glory and our joy, Amen

dependence upon god

But we are not independent. None of us are. We were not created to be independent. We were formed to be dependent on the One who made us, and we were re-created in Jesus Christ to be dependent on his grace.
— Paul David Tripp, *New Morning Mercies*

Father God, when we think we have it all together, when we think we can move forward in our own strength, remind us again that we are dependent upon You, that we need Your holy presence in our lives, that we require Your mercy and grace if we are to walk in Your will, if we are to complete the tasks You have set before us. Fill our words, both written and spoken, with Truth. *You* are Truth, Jesus. We live in a world pressed down by sin. Help us to be lights that cut through the darkness.

In the wonderful name of Jesus, Amen

free us from sin

My country,' tis of thee, sweet land of liberty, of thee I sing;
land where my fathers died, land of the pilgrims' pride, from
every mountainside let freedom ring!

Father God, one of Your primary purposes for Your people is to free us from physical oppression and to liberate us from spiritual bondage. On this day when Americans celebrate Independence Day, would You remind all of us of our utter dependence upon You to free us from the bondage of sin. Would You remind us to call upon You for every need in our lives. Would You help us to understand the true meaning of freedom.

Lord, we pray for the many needs represented by those who

read this prayer. We ask for healing for those of us who are sick in our bodies. We ask for peace for those of us with troubled hearts. And we ask for joy and thanksgiving to well up in our souls. May we know Jesus in a greater way today. May we live as if we truly believe that the Lord could return at any moment. May we feel the urgency of sharing the gospel of Jesus Christ, knowing that time is short. Give us Your strength and power to make a difference in this troubled world, Lord.

Amen and Amen

speak wisdom

It is absolutely clear that God has called you to a free life. Just make sure that you don't use this freedom as an excuse to do whatever you want to do and destroy your freedom. Rather, use your freedom to serve one another in love; that's how freedom grows. For everything we know about God's Word is summed up in a single sentence: Love others as you love yourself. That's an act of true freedom. If you bite and ravage each other, watch out—in no time at all you will be annihilating each other, and where will your precious freedom be then? (Galatians 5:13–15, The Message)

Father God, we are grateful for the freedoms we enjoy. We thank You for those who have fought for those freedoms to be preserved. But we acknowledge that we, as a people, are flawed, that we don't always do the right things. Forgive us, Lord, when we stray from Your righteous path.

Father, we know the importance of words, those spoken and those written. Would You help us to speak wisdom, through our writing, into our troubled world. Would You help us provide entertainment to relieve readers who feel overburdened by their cares. Would You help us to write peace and truth and justice. Would You help us ignite a great desire to know You and to walk with You.

We are Your servants, Lord. Guide us today.

prayer for labor day

. . .

the work of our hands

Whom have I in heaven but You? And besides You, I desire nothing on earth. My flesh and my heart may fail, But God is the strength of my heart and my portion forever. (Psalm 73:25–26, NASB95)
You are my God, and I give thanks to You; You are my God, I extol You. Give thanks to the Lord, for He is good; For His lovingkindness is everlasting. (Psalm 118:28–29, NASB95)

Almighty God, who spoke the world into being and who breathed life into man, there are many needs among Christian writers. Some of them are known to us. Most are not. But You, Lord, see all things. You hear the silent cries, and You are moved with compassion. We thank You for that, Father God. We are overwhelmed by the knowledge of Your love for us.

Lord, on this Labor Day, would You encourage us as we write. Infuse the work of our hands with Your divine words. Would You help us to hear Your voice, reminding us that we have the mind of Christ because we belong to Him. Would You touch the hearts that are hurting and bring rejoicing to those who have soaked their pillows with tears. Would you cause the lame to walk and the blind to see.

And finally, Lord, even if You do not answer our prayers the way we think You should or even the way we have wanted, may we be like Shadrach, Meshach, and Abednego and respond in our situation as they did in theirs, "Our God whom we serve is able to deliver us from the furnace of blazing fire; and He will deliver us out of your hand, O king. But even if He does not, let it be known to you, O king, that we are not going to serve your gods or worship the golden image that you have set up." Let us say as Job did, "Though He slay me, I will hope in Him."

Jesus, there is nothing here on earth we desire besides You. Blessed be the name of the Lord.

storms

Father God, today in America we are celebrating Labor Day, a day to honor the workers in our nation.

And today, we lift up prayers especially for everyone who is laboring in storm-ravished areas of the world. Give those workers strength and courage and wisdom. Let those who minister in Your name not only be Your hands and feet but give them those divine moments when they might speak Your words of truth and comfort into the lives of those who are hurting. Protect them from disease and from whatever dangers lurk in nature.

Lord, help our governments—local, state, and federal—to respond swiftly and responsibly to disaster. Bless those neighbors who have been helping others from the start. Comfort the families who have lost loved ones.

We ask it in Your mighty name, Amen

prayer for thanksgiving day

. . .

contentment

Gratitude is the fairest blossom which springs from the soul. — Henry Ward Beecher

Father God, we come to you on this Thanksgiving Day, asking that You would stir up our hearts in gratitude. Help us to be content whether we find ourselves in plenty or in want. Help us to remember that little is much if You are in it. May we be a blessing to those around us, by our actions and by our words and perhaps even by our silence.

Lord, we thank You for each and every one of the readers of our books and stories. Thank You that we are allowed to share truth with a world that is hurting. We thank You that You have a plan for each of our lives. You made us unique, and You have a purpose that is unique to each one of us. How wonderful to know that, Jesus! We glorify You!

Amen

guard our mouths

Finally, brethren, whatever is true, whatever is honorable, whatever is right, whatever is pure, whatever is lovely, whatever is of good repute, if there is any excellence and if anything worthy of praise, dwell on these things. (Philippians 4:8, NASB95)

Lord, we live in a culture where people say whatever they think or feel without regard to anyone around them. The culture tells us to criticize everyone from the President of our country on down to a janitor cleaning an office.

Help us, Lord. Put a guard over our mouths and teach us to dwell upon things that are true and honorable and right and pure and lovely and of good repute. Cultivate in us hearts that are full of thanksgiving instead of complaint. Forgive us for words carelessly spoken.

And, Lord, let us remember every single day to be a thankful people. Fill us with grace and gratitude.

In Your name, Amen

prayer for the christmas season

. . .

even so, come

Father God, in this blessed season of the year when we who believe honor the coming of Your Son Jesus to earth, we want to thank You for all You have done and for all You are doing in our lives and in the lives of those whom we love.

In Isaiah 30:8, it says, "Now go, write it on a tablet before them and inscribe it on a scroll, that it may serve in the time to come as a witness forever." We pray that this will be true of our own writing, Lord. May the stories we write serve as a witness to Your glory, to Your plan, to Your people, to Your power.

Your word also tells us that You long to be gracious to us and that You wait on high to have compassion on us. You, Father, are a God of justice. How blessed are all who long for You. At the sound of our cries, You are gracious. You hear our voices and answer us. You cause our ears to hear when You say, "This is the way, walk in it."

Thank You for the mercy and grace that is poured out upon us day by day, minute by minute. You alone are God, the One in whom we place our trust. Even so, come, Lord Jesus.

wonderful counselor

For a child will be born to us, a son will be given to us; And the government will rest on His shoulders; And His name will be called Wonderful Counselor, Mighty God, Eternal Father, Prince of Peace. There will be no end to the increase of His government or of peace, On the throne of David and over his kingdom, To establish it and to uphold it with justice and righteousness From then on and forevermore. The zeal of the Lord of hosts will accomplish this. (Isaiah 9:6–7, NASB95)

Father God, we have entered the season of Advent. While we celebrate the first Advent, we look with great anticipation for the Second Advent, for the Second Coming of Jesus. Two thousand years ago, You sent Your Son to fulfill the prophecies of old. We are so very thankful for all that Jesus accomplished on our behalf. But we long for the day when *all* of the prophecies will be fulfilled, completely fulfilled, when there will be no more tears, no more sorrow or sighing.

Lord, some of us are entering this Christmas season for the first time without someone we love. Would You touch and heal the grief in our hearts. Would You give us fresh hope and a new vision for the future.

Wonderful Counselor, Mighty God, Eternal Father, Prince of Peace, help us to make space for You in our lives in the weeks to come. Help us to be still and to listen to Your voice. Drive out the busyness and replace it with Your holy presence.

In the mighty name of Jesus we pray, Amen

reason for the season

Read Luke 2:1-14

Father God, it's nearly Christmas. Help us to stop in the midst of the hurry and bustle to remember again that Jesus is the Reason for the Season. Help us to see with new eyes the awe and wonder of the night of Christ's birth. Help us to forget our money worries, the stress, the concerns, and anything that might keep us from worshiping You with our whole heart, mind, and strength.

We pray especially for the prodigal children of all who read this prayer. Jesus, would You reach out to the prodigals and cause them to see You in a whole new light. Blind them with Your glory, at the same time opening their eyes to see! And Lord, if those prodigals are estranged from their families as well as from You, would You cause grace to flow, would You bring about forgiveness and peace, would You heal these families.

Lord, we also pray for those of us who have lost loved ones to death or divorce or anger during this past year. Would You surround us this Christmas and drive out all feelings of loneliness and of being alone. Would You cause us to feel Your presence from the moment we awaken to the moment we rest in slumber. And please help those of us who are surrounded with family and loved ones to remember those who have no one at Christmas. Make us a compassionate people, Lord.

O God of the heavenly hosts, show us the light of Your countenance. No matter what You ask of us, help us to respond to You as Mary responded to the angel who foretold the birth of Jesus: "Behold, the bondslave of the Lord; may it be done to me according to your word."

Glory to God in the highest, And on earth peace among men with whom He is pleased.

set our eyes on you

Lord Jesus, You stepped down into the darkness of this world because You love us. In this bustling, busy season, in this season that can be challenging and sad for many, would You remind us again and again why we celebrate Christmas. May our eyes be set upon You, Jesus. May we bask in Your light.

hope arise

Jesus, in this Advent season, cause hope to rise up inside of us once again. The hope of Your coming. Let us be like little children, holding our breath, awaiting that moment when we shall see You face to face.

If we are alone and missing loved ones, remind us how near You are. If we are overwhelmed with family and responsibilities, help us to find moments of peace to be with You. If we are ill, touch our bodies and bring healing. Whatever our condition, Lord, You are the answer. Our hope remains in You.

light of the world

There was the true Light which, coming into the world, enlightens every man. (John 1:9, NASB95)

King Jesus, You are the Light of the world. Whoever follows You will never walk in darkness. In this busy Christmas season, help us to illuminate the world around us with Your light. Help us to reflect Your glory and reveal the hope of life eternal in You. Help us to share with others the miracle that began in that manger so long ago.

In Your glorious name we pray, Amen

jesus, living word

Father God, we are in the midst of the hustle and bustle of the Christmas Season. As believers, we love to celebrate the birth of our Savior. But some of us are susceptible to the blues this time of year, too. Help us.

Lord, for those of us on tight deadlines who must write right through this blessed holiday, would You grant self-discipline and an increase in inspiration and a dose of unusual stamina.

Lord, for those of us who will miss loved ones this Christmas, would You give us extra love from other family and friends to ease us through those sad moments. Would You especially wrap us in Your arms and allow us to feel You carrying us through.

Lord, for those of us who are struggling financially, would You open new doors of opportunity for us to walk through. Would You grant us fresh hope for the coming new year.

Jesus, Living Word, today and throughout this holy season, would You make this verse from the written word come alive in our hearts in a new and glorious way:

For a child will be born to us, a son will be given to us; And the government will rest on His shoulders; And His name will be called Wonderful Counselor, Mighty God, Eternal Father, Prince of Peace.

Amen and Amen

sing in the night

*Afflictions cannot injure when we blend them with submission
... Every now and then I meet someone who sings in affliction, and then
I thank God for my own circumstance as well as his. There is never a
song more beautiful than that which is sung in the night.* — Henry
Ward Beecher

Father God, today we ask that You make each one of us into
Christ-followers who can, will, and do sing in the night. We
acknowledge that nothing enters our lives that is not caused or
allowed by You for the purpose of refining us and making us
more like Your Son. Sometimes that is uncomfortable. Sometimes
that is painful. Dreams die. Loved ones fall ill. We struggle with
choices. We feel we have no choices.

We are Christians who write. You have given us the desire to
write for You. Help us to "sing songs in the night" through our
writing. Help us to write stories that will encourage and lift up
those who read our words. And, Lord, as we prepare to celebrate
the birth of Jesus in a world that grows more ignorant of You by
the day, would You fill us with Your Holy Spirit and empower us
to shine truth wherever we go.

In Christ's blessed name we pray, Amen

prayer for the year's end

. . .

fear not!

Father God, for some writers, this has been a difficult year, personally and/or professionally. Some have lost loved ones. Some have lost jobs or contracts. Some have lost creativity. Some have lost joy.

This has been a difficult year for many in our nation and around the world as well. Sometimes it's hard not to give into fear, hard not to feel overwhelmed and even hopeless.

But You, Lord, say to us, "Fear not!" Help us to grasp Your unshakable commitment to our well-being. You have not given us a spirit of fear but a Spirit of power, love, and a sound mind. We can be confident because we belong to You. We can cry out to you, "Abba, Father," and You are right there beside us. You are our hope.

Teach us to listen to You so that we will know when to move forward and when to wait. Your word tells us that the sheep know the shepherd's voice. Help us to recognize our Shepherd's voice even when we are surrounded by the noise of this world.

Father, as we look into the months ahead, would You make it a time when we serve You in new, exciting, meaningful, deeper ways. Would You grant us confidence and wisdom. Would You make us a powerful force in our spheres of influence. And would You remind us, when the time is right, to come away and rest. Fill us up, Lord, with your Holy Spirit, so that we can pour out upon those around us. Make us a generous people. Help us to give not only out of our abundance but out of our little. Help us to let go of things and take hold of people.

Lord, we give You the books and articles and blogs and anything else that we are supposed to write for You. We offer them to You to do with what You will. And we do this in the name of Your Son, Jesus.

quit striving

Abba Father, another year is at an end. They fly by so quickly, and so many of us feel tired and worn out by life itself. Some of us feel like failures, in our personal lives, in our spiritual lives, in our writing lives.

Lord, would You take us into Your lap and remind us how much You love us ... just as we are. Would You allow us to feel Your arms around us and remind us of all that You have done for us out of love. Would You help us quit striving to please and instead enjoy being Your children.

Blessed Savior, we have no light apart from You. Light our way into the new year, we pray.

afterword

Thank you for joining me in these prayers from my heart. I hope they blessed and encouraged you. As a writer, I know that words matter. They can bring hope and comfort or spread fear and despair. I desire the former.

If you're curious about the books that I've written, turn the page to see a list of titles of current and upcoming Christian fiction.

Robin

also by robin lee hatcher

stand alone titles

I'll Be Seeing You

Words Matter

Make You Feel My Love

Even Forever

An Idaho Christmas

Here in Hart's Crossing

The Victory Club

Beyond the Shadows

Catching Katie

Whispers From Yesterday

The Shepherd's Voice

Ribbon of Years

Firstborn

The Forgiving Hour

Heart Rings

A Wish and a Prayer

When Love Blooms

A Carol for Christmas

Return to Me

Loving Libby

Wagered Heart

The Perfect Life

Speak to Me of Love

Trouble in Paradise

Another Chance to Love You

Bundle of Joy

coming to america series

Dear Lady

Patterns of Love

In His Arms

Promised to Me

where the heart lives series

Belonging

Betrayal

Beloved

books set in kings meadow

A Promise Kept

Love Without End

Whenever You Come Around

I Hope You Dance

Keeper of the Stars

books set in thunder creek

You'll Think of Me

You're Gonna Love Me

sisters of bethlehem springs series

A Vote of Confidence

Fit to Be Tied

A Matter of Character

legacy of faith series

Who I Am with You

Cross My Heart

How Sweet It Is

For more information about me and my books, visit www. robinleehatcher.com

Made in the USA
Middletown, DE
03 March 2024

50750662R00068